The Comfort Dog
Gave Me Pink Eye

The Comfort Dog Gave Me Pink Eye

Lessons From the Book of Esther

COURTNEY L. BURNS

Foreword by Steven J. Buuck

Photos by Jill Heupel at Jill Heupel Photography

RESOURCE *Publications* • Eugene, Oregon

THE COMFORT DOG GAVE ME PINK EYE
Lessons From the Book of Esther

The events and conversations in this book have been set down to the best of the author's ability, although some names and details have been changed to protect the privacy of individuals. Some things may be embellished, as the author is known for flair and exaggeration.

Resource Publications
An Imprint of Wipf and Stock Publishers
199 W. 8th Ave., Suite 3
Eugene, OR 97401

www.wipfandstock.com

PAPERBACK ISBN: 978-1-7252-7435-8
HARDCOVER ISBN: 978-1-7252-7436-5
EBOOK ISBN: 978-1-7252-7437-2

Manufactured in the U.S.A.   09/14/20

For my godfather, Chuck Ackley.
You are an example of what it means
to walk faithfully, love humbly, and boldly live your purpose.
I thank my God when I remember you.

And who knows but that you have come
to your royal position for such a time as this?

—ESTHER 4:14B

Contents

Foreword

I AM BLESSED TO serve as the Chief Executive Officer at Faith Lutheran Middle School & High School, one of the largest Christian schools in the United States serving nearly 2,000 students in grades 6–12. More importantly, *I'm afraid of dogs*. In fact, I've spent the majority of my life avoiding them. My fear started when I was 10 years old, and I watched in horror while a friend of mine got bit by a German shepherd while on my paper route in northeast Portland, Oregon. It escalated over the years on my paper route; I recall countless times that I peddled as fast as I could down streets with dogs chasing me. I would attempt to gather enough speed so I could lift my feet onto the handlebars to avoid my ankles getting bit. The pinnacle (perhaps valley is a better word) occurred one day in a trailer park as I was about to throw the *Oregon Journal* over a short fence and onto the small porch of one of my customers, a dog owner. That day, however, the elderly woman asked me to bring the paper to her as she sat on her chair on the tiny porch. "He's never bit anyone," she promised, "bring me the paper." Seconds after venturing inside her gate, her dog bit me on my lower leg. Those formative experiences with dogs have led me through life frightened by the sight and sounds of dogs.

That said, one can imagine my initial reaction when our Middle School Director of Guidance, Courtney Burns, first suggested to me in the fall of 2016 that our school should get a comfort dog; I steadfastly resisted her idea for a full year. That all changed when I saw how a team of comfort dogs helped change the depressed and subdued mood hanging over our campus in the days immediately following the horrific mass shooting on October 1, 2017 at the Route 91 Harvest musical festival in our beautiful city, Las Vegas. Two students and one recent alum were shot that fateful Sunday night, while other students and faculty were there to experience the unimaginable fear and panic that ensued from the gruesome sights and sounds.

An emotional cloud hung over our campus on Monday and part of Tuesday until the Lutheran Church Charities flew in from around the United States and came to campus on Tuesday with almost a dozen trained comfort dogs. Students, faculty, and staff flocked to these dogs. Instantly, students who had been inconsolable smiled and laughed for the first time. I witnessed first hand what Courtney had been trying to convince me of for more than a year. Courtney and her family immediately provided a plan that I simply could not refuse. They absorbed the majority of costs for Esther including training her, housing her, and bringing her to school each day.

Esther has become an invaluable employee, a social media sensation, and frequent guest on local television stations in Las Vegas. She has won the hearts of our students, faculty, staff, visitors, and followers around the world. Yes, she's even won me over. She is the one dog in the world I trust to be on our campus. In fact, "Esther's Garden", a gated area for her to call her own, is immediately attached to the outside of my office so I often see her out my window. My heart no longer races when I see her; my heart smiles with unbridled joy. I truly believe Esther was indeed "born for such a time as this."

You, my dear reader, are in for a treat. Courtney Burns is one of those rare people whose writing I can't wait to read. Whether it's a Facebook post, a blog, an email at work, or a book about how a dog can transform a school community, she has a true gift for wit, sarcasm, insight, and humor. Moreover, she is an expert on this subject who is a sought after speaker at national conferences. Courtney is singularly responsible for introducing Esther to our campus. Esther was Courtney's idea, and Esther remains Courtney's responsibility and passion.

I have personally seen how a comfort dog can bring healing, love, joy, and peace to a school. My initial skepticism has been replaced with enthusiastic endorsement. With more than 56 million students attending elementary, middle school, and high school in the United States alone this year, this book will give educators, lawmakers, parents, and students unique insights into how to bring the indelible impact of a comfort animal to the beautiful people they serve.

Steven J. Buuck, PhD
Chief Executive Officer
Faith Lutheran Middle School & High School
Fabulous Las Vegas, Nevada

Introduction

I WROTE THE BULK of this book during a time of unspeakable tragedy and uncommon hope. Esther Bean the Comfort Dog came into my life in the wake of a mass shooting as my school struggled to find ways to meet the needs of traumatized students. She completed her training in a dismal two year period surrounded by death and despair. I truly believed that time in my life would be the most chaos and tragedy I would ever bear witness to. Yet as I prepare to submit this story and write the words of this introduction years later, I sit in my house during another unprecedented crisis; the coronavirus quarantine of 2020. We are less than one month in and while I am sure as time goes on it will get a fancier name, for now this is how we refer to it. I sat in a Zoom call with my work husband, Dan, this morning where he asked me if I ever imagined we would live in a time that actually made us nostalgic for the sadness and chaos of the 2017/2018 school year.

I didn't. But he is right. In dealing with the tragedy of that year we banded together and pressed on, firm in our calling and the knowledge that we were working to bring healing. Today we sit isolated, craving both connection and a light at the end of the tunnel.

Like most of America, I intended to use this time in lockdown to get remarkably fit, organize my house, and master a new life skill. The memes swirl around taunting us that if we don't capitalize on the lockdown to get better, that is on us, because it means we never lacked time and we only lacked discipline. This is unfortunate because also like most of America I am working on gaining the Quarantine 15, my closets are in the same disarray they were when this all began, and I am probably dumber and definitely more anxious for the time I've spent scrolling on social media. I have managed to maintain a daily study of the Bible, either over Zoom with colleagues or on my own. And as I always do in times of stress I returned again to the book of Esther.

For years I've believed that the main lessons of the book of Esther center around courage in faith and rising to one's calling; topics I spent years exploring as I struggled to unravel this book. Of course, these are the lessons I was drawn toward. We all want to be champions for the right and stand boldly in the truth. We want to change history with the arrogant assurance that God is on our side. How comforting to call on Him when we are trying to draw courage; believing that God standing behind us makes us invincible as we ride into battle. Furthermore, when we do win it serves to underline our belief that God is backing us, the irresistible pull of being David against whichever Goliath you are facing.

Is there anything more empowering than the belief that God placed you in a moment, equipped you to handle it, and has your back?

While the Old Testament book of Esther is notable for many reasons, theologians frequently return to the fact that it is one of only two books of the Bible that never mention God. This is pretty weighty when you consider that the people in the book of Esther are facing a genocide at the mercy of a drunken king and a diabolical sidekick. The book reads like a soap opera and even the most casual reader of the Bible has to wonder why God isn't showing up to put a stop to nonsense, like He does in so many places throughout the Old Testament.

The fear that God is not present is something we can all relate to wrestling with during times of crisis. As I sit in quarantine today wondering just how many people are going to die, how total the economic collapse will be, and if we will ever get to go back to school it is tempting to wonder where God is in all of this. And as I clumsily fumbled my way through the first few years of Esther the dog's life, in the wake of so much tragedy, I certainly did question God and why I struggled at times to feel His presence. Throughout the book of Esther, although God is not called by name or depicted in scenes, it is clear that He is still in control and still working behind it all. Today He continues to run the show, placing people in specific situations at specific times to work for His glory.

Not familiar with the Biblical story of Esther? We will get there.

Not familiar with the story of Esther Bean, the orange Comfort Dog? Less historic and impressive, significantly derpier, but we will cover that, too.

Feeling uncertain, overwhelmed, underprepared, and ill equipped? Purposeless, burned out, or unworthy? Pull up a chair, friend. You've found your people.

Way back in 483 B.C, a young girl named Esther faced the crisis of the genocide of her people. We are currently facing a pandemic unlike anything the world has seen before. I have no idea what the future holds. There is fear, uncertainty, and sadness in even the most faithful of the people I know.

Today, I sit quietly and consider that there is one lesson that I did not spend nearly enough time on and that is the most important one of all; the times when it appears God is absent or invisible He remains utterly invincible. God has worked silently behind the scenes to orchestrate every event in history. He is present and powerful in today's times as well. This hidden God is our God. The God of all of us humble and fearful people, while we just try to make sense of the chaos around us.

Chapter 1

A Dark Night in Las Vegas

THIS IS THE STORY of a fuzzy orange dog, a terrifying shooting, and finding the balance between grace and accountability. It is also about God finding ways to use horrible tragedies and broken people to spread love. As every working mother knows, the moments stolen before the sun comes up are usually the finest and the most productive of the day. This book is a product of those fleeting moments, often tearfully scribed as the magnitude of what had unfolded lay before me.

Perhaps that is a bit dramatic. It may be more accurate to say that it was often tearfully scribed due to stress and exhaustion. And it was often resentfully written when I had to choose between writing, a twenty minute affair with the snooze button, or a quick run that might take the jiggle out of my belly. However it unfolded, I felt compelled to share these thoughts with anyone considering a therapy dog program, a career in ministry, having children, working with children, and/or growing their community beyond themselves. And also to the people who struggle with taking grace when it is offered or finding humility in broken moments. Especially to those of you, for you are my people and we are going to learn to admit we are human and get through this together.

I love God, I love children, I do my best with adults. Try as I might to approach parents with open arms and loving hearts, my own social anxiety often grips me to the point that returning simple phone calls can cause a deep burn in my stomach lining. I'm working on that. But kids? Kids are way easier. This makes being a counselor in a gorgeous Lutheran school in Las Vegas a great fit for me. I took a very winding and unusual career path to get to where I am today, one that some of my high school students delight in hearing as they sweat choosing a major in college or feel like everyone else has it more together than they do.

I think the biggest myth is that kids are supposed to know what they want to do with their lives when they are still teenagers. Growing up in a small town in Michigan, I had no idea. I was a less than stellar student with a chaotic home and little idea how to navigate life. As a middle aged woman, I somewhat give the appearance of having my life together, sometimes. My students are typically relieved to find out that wasn't always the case. They hunker down to hear about how I drifted into college, the first in my family to do so, mostly because my friends were all going and I didn't want to be left out. People in my family just didn't go to universities. They worked in retail or for General Motors just until it was time to collect a meager pension. Weekends were filled with beer drinking, BBQs, and trips to tiny cabins in Northern Michigan. Education beyond my high school diploma was never an expectation placed on me and it wasn't something I had given a lot of thought to. I toured zero colleges, had no plan for a major, and went to Michigan State because, again, it was where my friends went. Fortunately, this is the best college in Michigan, so that worked out. I also took out an obscene amount of loans, as I was putting myself through on my own and worked an unsettling number of jobs. Unrelated, I failed basic math more times than I usually will admit. Ok, three. I failed basic math three times. There were a few points that I worried that I wouldn't ever graduate because I somehow had never learned math in high school.

With no idea what I wanted to do and no guidance from anyone, I started my college career as a finance major. Admittedly, this was a bold move for someone who could not pass the no credit introductory math class nor has any actual interest in economics. It sounded highly intelligent and that was good enough for me. I wasn't sure what one would do with a finance degree, but I was optimistic it would work out. That confidence lasted all the way into my first microeconomics class where I finally had to face the fact that I was a fish out of water. Looking back, my undergraduate years are a blur of feeling like I was in over my head, crying myself to sleep over only having five dollars to last the week, and working, working, working, and working. I was consistently jealous of my friends who had rent paid by their parents and a monthly allowance check to rely on. It was a curious mix of being thrilled at my independence and resentful that I had to work so hard.

Outside of class, I sold tuxedos at a little formal wear shop for a few years, which is a great way to repeatedly get sexually harassed as a young woman. Disheveled groomsmen reeking of Bud Light and body odor would repeatedly cock an eyebrow and ask if I was going to take an inseam measurement or slur through inviting me to the wedding while picking up tuxes the night before. I would hold my breath and try to measure them as quickly and accurately as possible. The day after the wedding they would return the tuxes in a knotted trash bag and sheepishly advise me not to open the bag. The real punishment was that I had to account for all of the tuxedo pieces, so I always had to open the bag. It was disgusting, but served to prepare me for the horrors of parenting toddlers with the flu.

But seriously. Gentlemen. If you ever find yourself in the kind of emotional place where you believe the woman measuring you for a suit is touching you because she is interested in you romantically, please stop and reevaluate.

I digress.

I also tended the bar at a tiny dive where locals could pony up seventy cents for a shell of Miller Light. Here I oddly got hit on less than at the tuxedo shop. Eventually I landed a gig as a swim coach. On the pool deck I realized how much I loved working with kids. I also met my husband there, thanks to a blind date set up by my diving coach. It's funny in hindsight how pivotal that little part time job coaching swimming really was in my life. I know God plants us in different places according to His plan, but I never thought the grimy pool deck of a Lansing, Michigan high school would be the place that altered the course of my life. I changed my major to psychology in order to graduate in close to four years and investigated the alternate route to licensure for teachers. Graduation day was one of the proudest of my life. It was an accomplishment I had done completely on my own and one that no one could ever take away.

One of the parents on my swim team was the superintendent for a local school district. He approached me about filling in for a special education teacher out on medical leave and helped me navigate all of the red tape. Just a few years earlier I would never have imagined myself in the classroom, but it turned out that I really loved teaching special education and the times I had with those kids. I enjoyed the rhythm of the school year and the structure of the school day, even if I am kind of terrible at sticking to a routine.

After two years of teaching, things seemed to be set. I enjoyed being in the classroom, even if the school I taught at was inner city and a little terrifying. I learned how to make oatmeal in the crockpot so that my students would have a hot breakfast and how to tell if the drug dogs were coming based on the amount of weed dumped in my classroom trash can. Breaking up fights was commonplace and I became pretty adept at that as well. I had also picked up another part time job at the juvenile detention center. My students were there so often, with me trailing behind to advocate for them, that they eventually just hired me. The handsome firefighter from my blind date had turned into a serious boyfriend and I just knew that he was going to be the one I married. I continued to coach swimming for both club and high school teams. Life was busy, but it was fairly pleasant.

Until the day that handsome firefighter from Lansing, Michigan decided that he wanted to become a handsome police officer in Las Vegas. Early mid-life crisis or not, it was the ultimate bait and switch. Too in love with him to turn back now, I married him and found myself in a large city where I had never had any interest in living. I taught in a small Lutheran school for ten years and took out another obscene round of student loans to obtain a masters in school counseling. I also had two adorable babies during that time. The years sped by in a blur of working, running marathons, trying to raise two kids, and constantly adjusting to my husband's ever changing schedule. Just when I thought I couldn't take much more, the timing must have been just right because God placed me in the amazing school I am at now, in the job that I love doing.

By this point in the story, my students are usually a little less impressed. They are typically kids who are deciding between business and law at Ivy League schools.

"See?" I often gesture to my tiny, cluttered, windowless office filled with particle board furniture I found at IKEA. "One day this kind of happiness could be yours!" They are typically polite enough not to laugh at me, which I appreciate.

I also really really love dogs, having owned them my whole life starting in my childhood with a poorly trained rescue Springer Spaniel named Gertie. Gertie is most famous for discovering and consuming a giant bag of chocolate chips, then vomiting them up all over the living room the day after new white carpeting was installed. As an adult, I begged my husband for a pug for reasons that I can't quite remember now. We got Butters, who immediately became loyal only to my husband, Zack. In an effort to get a dog I could pet, we adopted another pug named Peanut who was the worst dog ever and only wanted to be with Butters. Both pugs lived for over 16 years, because pugs are aliens who will sometimes shoot liquid from their faces and also pee in your shoes if you upset them.

After failing to connect with either pug, it was obviously time to start having children in the hopes that someone would finally need me. My son, Evan, was born first and followed by his sister, Petey, a few years later. The pugs peed on both of them while they were learning to crawl because, again, pugs are the worst. We brought home Maeby, the giant gentle English Mastiff when the kids were still little. She is the dog of my heart and was impeccably trained in just two short, but humiliating, years. We would haul her to an obedience class full of eager German Shepherds where cues would be given and the other dogs would spring into action. Maeby more often rolled around on the ground screaming or simply refused to get up. We congratulated ourselves on having a dog who would never run away.

By the time Maeby was about three I began to lobby the CEO of my school to allow us to get a therapy dog on campus. It was a brilliant plan. The dog could work with the counselors, the special education department, be available to classrooms, and go on home visits when families suffer a trauma or loss. The big problem? My CEO feared and loathed dogs with the same level of intensity that I loved them and was willing to forgive the occasional urination on a baby. For years we had a standoff. I would work on well thought out plans that he would systematically veto every time. For a while I pitched a therapy pig program based off of a program an airport was attempting. Turns out pigs love therapy work. He rubbed his chin a little on that idea, interested in the niche marketing that could result from a pig on campus wearing our school's gear. It was enough to encourage me to start communicating with a pig breeder out of Utah, until he vetoed that idea as well.

On September 28th, 2017, I took yet another run at convincing him the dog was a good idea. I cited quotes from a Lutheran college counselor who had a successful program and talked about a kennel just outside of Las Vegas that bred hypo-allergenic working dogs. This time he told me that he was "98% sold on the idea." While this was encouraging, I am fairly certain that he said this the same way that I tell my kids "maybe" when they beg to do something that sounds torturous or involves indoor trampolines.

A few days later 1 October happened. If you are unfamiliar, a psychopath rained semi-automatic gunfire down on a crowd of country music concert goers outside of the Mandalay Bay. It remains the largest mass shooting on American soil in history. Everyone in Vegas has a 1 October story. It is our 9–11; we all remember where we were. I was in bed, because it was after 9pm and I have the sleep habits of a Golden Girl. My husband, that handsome firefighter turned Las Vegas Metropolitan policeman, woke me up to tell me that someone was shooting into a crowd from the Mandalay Bay. He had his police radio turned on as he prepared to head to the scene and we heard the famous "breach. . .breach. . ..breach. . ." as SWAT blew open the door to the madman's hotel room.

Zack quickly dressed and packed his things, kissed me goodbye, and headed to the Strip. At that point we had no idea what was happening down there, if this was a terrorist attack, if there would be more violence, how many were dead or injured. Preliminary reports over the radio suggested that shots were being fired in other casinos and this was the work of more than one attacker. It was truly the unknown.

I have to admit in this moment that I've always rolled my eyes a little at some of the emotional posturing of first responder spouses.

Ok, a lot. I've rolled them a lot.

Yes, law enforcement life is stressful in a number of ways; the shift work, the changing schedules, the fact that no matter what your day brings your spouse will always have a story that tops it, and that you can never trust what tale they will tell at dinner parties. I've often complained that I will never once ever be successful in getting sympathy for being the one to have the worse day. Even with all of Zack's stories, the number of times I've truly feared for his safety are far outweighed by normal days. It deeply saddens me when I hear wives tell stories about their kids crying in fear when dad leaves for work or about how the emotional tension of the entire house shoots up when a call out happens. In many conversations with other spouses I've been surprised at how the law enforcement job defines the identity and mood of the entire family.

Perhaps it's a little simplistic, but I've always subscribed to the belief that God numbers our days before we are born and so it does not matter if you are a cop or an accountant. I have friends who worry about having arguments with their police spouses, afraid that something will happen while they are at work and they will have parted on an argument. I understand the logic of that thinking, but I don't believe that it is sustainable as a marriage model. I love the man dearly, I pray for his safety, yet I am still going to be super annoyed if he forgets to pick the kids up or start the crockpot. He doesn't get a pass from life because he's basically a superhero. By the time 1 October happened Zack had added 15 years of police experience to the 6 years he had worked as a firefighter and promoted his way up to Lieutenant. I had kissed him good-bye thousands of times. That was the first time I had ever done so with a flicker of fear in my stomach, with some knowledge about what he was going to face. Startling as that fear was, in the quiet moments after he left I realized that I had been right in letting normal life happen for all of those years and not living in fear of all of the what ifs that his job could bring. We lived a normal life, with normal arguments and normal tension, and we both were confident in what we meant to each other. Our kids did not feel the stress or fear of his job and were proud of him. As much as I didn't know what he was heading into, I also felt an undercurrent of peace that he would be ok.

As I was reflecting on all of this my phone began pinging with texts from students reporting that we had kids in attendance at the concert and that word was one had been shot. The other administrators and I began a group chat and started trying to sort things out and make sense of what was happening. Student information can be unintentionally unreliable under normal circumstances and we didn't want to jump into believing all of the rumors were true. I sat on the couch with my phone in my hand, my computer in my lap, and the TV muted. The scene playing out before me was horrific, bodies everywhere and people fleeing in terror. I strained to see anyone I recognized in the crowds and my stomach dropped when I saw officers that we knew heroically shielding civilians with their bodies. As the hours ticked by and morning crept in, we began to determine that we had two students shot and both were still alive. We believed we had at least ten students in attendance, plus faculty, and innumerable parents.

Zack eventually texted that he was done at the Strip and was heading to Mesquite with SWAT to begin investigating the shooter's house. I knew that text, the first in many hours, would be the last communication we would probably have for quite some time. The police department would be heading to an emergency roster, meaning that everyone works twelve hours every single day. Law enforcement families hunkered down to weather the storm, offering to help each other with rides and childcare. I woke my own kids up and told them just that there had been a shooting on the Strip and their dad had to go to work. Accustomed to him being constantly called out, they were not phased and went about the morning routine of bickering and hunting for breakfast. I was careful to keep the television turned off so that they wouldn't be exposed to images of the night before.

Going into school was extra surreal. Like most Americans, I've seen scenes of tragedy on the news but always in other places and with other people, never along streets familiar to me. Perhaps I've wondered idly how normalcy continues after these events, but I had never given it too much thought. Surreal is the only word to describe it. Everything is the same, but remarkably different at the same time. For us, it was Homecoming Week and that Monday was pajama day. Students and faculty members wandered around dazedly, absurdly wearing jammies and distractedly hugging each other. The phones were ringing off the hook with parents wanting to tell us what they had heard about students at the concert or letting us know that they were keeping their kids home from school. The high school director of guidance (and my official work husband), Dan, and I sat in his office before school drinking coffee and staring at each other. Other administrators trickled in.

Do we send a mass email or use the all contact feature on the phones to tell parents that we still have school? Should that be our first communication? Should we gather all of the students first block and pray together? Should we send something out? What do we even say about something like this? As a school we were prepared for fires, active shooters on campus, school cancellations, and dealing with the death of community members. But this? We ultimately decided to proceed with the day; gathering the students in the morning, giving faculty guidance in how to handle these conversations with the kids, and canceling the evening's Homecoming Lip Sync competition.

Amazingly, eight of the students in attendance at the concert the night before came to school. Only the two who were currently hospitalized did not attend. We sat and we cried and we prayed. I held their hands and tried not to focus on the purple Route 91 concert bracelets they still wore. I heard their stories and my heart broke at the devastation they had witnessed and the terror they had survived. A pall lay over both our campus and our entire city. I still struggle to wrap my head around the damage and the devastation that one man was able to cause. Romans 5:20 continued to play through my mind. . .."but where sin abounds, grace abounds *much more*." We know that earth is often frightening and always sinful, but that the grace of God can comfort and heal all things. I reminded myself and my students again and again that no matter how out of control and scary things may be feeling, God is sovereign, present, and in control. The grace of God is much greater than the most terrible thing that man can do. While I believed this wholeheartedly, and still do, I could tell that my kids needed some physically present comfort to go along with the spiritual comfort.

Desperate to find a way to help, I reached out to the Lutheran Church Charities Comfort Dogs to see if they could send a few of their adorable Golden Retrievers to our campus. I had been in touch with the director earlier in the year as part of my research for my September dog proposal. I was so grateful to rediscover that contact card in my desk drawer. The LCC dogs and their handlers fly all over the country responding to crisis and I was told that they would try to have a few dogs on our campus the next day. The dogs are so sweet and so well trained for situations like this; I was cautiously optimistic that even if they couldn't heal everyone they could at least lighten the mood if through nothing else than the novelty of dogs at school. Also, is there anything better than the idea of a troop of fluffy golden dogs mobilizing to respond to crisis? The herd of them boarding the plane together ready to take care of business? I love it.

Still, heading home from school that day felt like wading through water. The edges of everything were fuzzy, things were off kilter. My husband wasn't going to be coming home anytime soon and it felt wrong to have to make dinner and check homework and drive kids to practices. It was hard to breathe and didn't seem right that all normalcy wasn't just suspended. It felt like we should get a trauma pass to stay home and wear sweatpants and eat carbs. I went through the motions of the evening while returning a constant stream of texts from coworkers, students, school parents, and concerned friends and family from different parts of the country. It was an exhausting and endless blur of assuring and attempting to be reassured.

My kids picked their way through dinner, feeling the effects of the tension in the air and uncertain how to respond. I was careful to continue to keep the televisions off, trying to limit the images they saw and the rhetoric they heard. They were used to their dad coming home after they went to bed and leaving before they woke, so while his absence wasn't stressful they weren't used to me being so distracted. My head was full of a running commentary of the day and I heard very few of the words they spoke. I tucked them in, kissed them goodnight, and prayed desperately for guidance in how to move forward and serve those around me. As the morning of October 3rd dawned it felt as though everyone in Vegas was running on empty, blindly moving about in a state of shock.

Chapter 2

Waiting on Esther Bean

SHORTLY AFTER I ARRIVED at work the next morning one of my girls who had been at the concert showed up in my office, crying so hard that I couldn't understand her. She cried and cried while I did my best to reassure her that she was safe. The front office rang in, interrupting to tell me that the dogs were out front.

"C'mon," I told her. "Let's go see if it helps to pet a dog."

I expected two or three dogs and was excited to see them. I was stunned when my student and I opened the door to find twelve smiling Golden Retrievers wagging tails and waiting for us. The girl let out a shriek and promptly disappeared into a pile of dogs. She emerged, smiling and coated in dog hair, a few minutes later. I named her student ambassador to the dogs and tasked her with guiding dogs and handlers around campus for the day. The other girls from the concert trickled in to hug dogs and the shift in the atmosphere was palpable. The dogs began to make the rounds, greeting children and adults alike.

After the last bell rang my CEO and I stood in the campus amphitheater watching grinning children covered in blonde fur race from dog to dog. The air felt lighter and laughter rang out. Even my girls from the concert were smiling and chatting with the dogs' handlers. Things felt normal for a few minutes; maybe even better than normal.

Steve sighed heavily. "Ok," he said. "I get it now. You can get a dog."

I'm sure he said other things, but I didn't hear any of them. I stood there for as short of a time as was socially acceptable when dealing with one's boss, then sprinted back to my office to quietly buy a dog. I still wasn't in regular contact with Zack, who was working an exhausting number of hours. We were communicating sporadically via text message, so I sent him a short note and let him spend the next few days trying to decide if I was kidding or not. I figured he would eventually get on board with our new family member when we eventually saw each other again.

The decision about where to purchase the puppy was an easy one. I had been in contact with the owner of 4E Kennels in Pahrump, about an hour outside of Vegas, for quite a while. Jeannette at 4E was known for breeding outstanding Goldendoodles. I didn't particularly like Goldendoodles, but they are considered to be hypoallergenic. A few members of the administration team are allergic enough to dogs that it came up every time we discussed starting a therapy dog program.

I'd been hassling Jeannette for a few months about a slightly older puppy named Diana that the kennel was on the fence about keeping or selling. After a great deal of back and forth, she ultimately decided to keep Diana for herself. I called Jeannette that day and asked her if I could be placed onto a waiting list for a litter that was going to be born in November. Feeling bad about backing out on Diana and the magnitude of what we were dealing with at Faith, this gorgeous woman agreed to move me to the top of the list for a new litter they were expecting.

At that point in time facility dogs were a novelty. The institutions that did have them did the responsible thing; they purchased a fully grown and completely trained dog. These working dogs will report for duty, passive and dedicated to serving. We saw the level of obedience in all of the LCC dogs who came to campus. Once, one of the pack barked. It was just a little bark and he looked surprised, like it had just slipped out before he could stop it. The other dogs instantly moved away from him in unison, as though they were trying to disassociate themselves from the barker, who looked properly ashamed of himself. Other than that one small leaked bark, not a single dog came close to stepping out of line all day. There was no barking, peeing, leash pulling, or distraction. Yes, getting a fully trained therapy dog would have made a lot of sense. Instead, we brought home a puppy. I had a vision of the puppy growing up around campus and being a part of our school culture, which is super unique but came with its own set of problems. The excitement over a new furry baby let me completely gloss over logically anticipating those problems.

The time between the day I paid the deposit for a dog and when the litter was actually born passed very quickly. The agony of 1 October still hung over both our campus and our entire city. We continued to identify families within our community who had been impacted. A local youth football coach, who was also an off duty police officer, had been killed that evening leaving several of our students deeply grieving. Kids trickled in telling tales of trying to locate parents who had been in attendance or of the loss of family friends. We tried to triage as much as we could and did our very best to keep track of who was affected. The students who had attended the concert were not doing well and the rest of the student body struggled to empathize or to support them. It seemed like the ripple of trauma widened as each day passed.

Adding to the stress of our PTSD afflicted students was the fact that we had begun major construction on various campus expansion projects. Typically, big campus projects bring excitement from both students and staff, and one of this year's projects was particularly exciting; a full working greenhouse to expand our science department, provide interesting activities for our special needs students, and generate fresh produce for the local food pantry. However, sporadic jackhammering and the accompanying construction noises repeatedly triggered the girls who survived the concert and I spent many days with a pile of crying and shaking girls in my office. This in turn raised the anxiety levels across the campus and I soon found all of my anxiety prone kids and faculty flaring up and needing more care. The other counselors and I would grimly nod at each other as we arrived in the morning, knowing that we had no idea what the day would bring or control over the events. A surprise fire drill, a showing of a WW2 clip in history class, anything and nothing could spark the debilitating symptoms of PTSD.

Those of us who are church workers will often acknowledge that we can't imagine doing the work that we do anywhere else. I've always believed that to be true. When I taught in the public school for a few years it was a struggle to not be able to pray with the kids and to not be able to fall back on my faith when faced with hard questions and hurting people. After transitioning from teacher to counselor, I was even more grateful to work in a setting where I could rely on the Truth when working with kids. Sometimes we enter into peaceful seasons both personally and professionally. The years leading up to 1 October were that kind of a season for me. Things were going well for my family and I loved my job and the people I saw every day. I felt useful and challenged in my ministry, but not overly burdened or overwhelmed.

During those seasons of peace, the joy in working in a Christian school doesn't necessarily diminish, but it can become somewhat superficial.

"I love working in a Lutheran school!" I would think this as I watched the Christmas trees get lit around campus and listened to the gorgeous music during advent chapel services. No matter where you are in your faith, you can't help but get the warm fuzzies when holiday traditions happen. Everyone is a sucker for a Christmas tree and caroling.

"I can't imagine working anywhere else." I would pat myself on the back for being a part of a place that made mission work a priority. Our school's actual mission statement is "Everyone prepared! Everyone saved!," the exclamation points serving to highlight the fervor with which we have accepted our mission. We work to grow and expand and bring as many as possible into the Faith Family joyfully preparing them for life on earth and, most importantly, eternal life to follow.

In these periods of peace, it's easy to get complacent, to forget exactly who we are and whose we are. I have found that when I am not under direct duress, I can become really avoidant. I joke that I will do a crisis all day long, give me something huge and traumatic and I will stay calm and steady. Give me a normal day and a few phone messages from parents angry about trivial things and I will shrink up into a ball and begin to doubt if I was ever any good at this job in the first place. Enough small conflict and I will escalate into a vortex of self doubt and try to work out any way I can in my head to avoid dealing with the resolutions. Simply put, I start sweating the small stuff. All of the small stuff. I allow it to loom large in my mind, larger than it deserves, and I get oddly burned out. It has cheered and disheartened me to learn that I am not alone in feeling this way. Turns out there are a good many of us who are willing to panic about the little things and lay awake at night stewing over social mishaps and minor disagreements. There's nothing like a solid round of beating yourself up over a human mistake. Sound familiar?

I'm not proud of it. Being called to ministry is hard work. Working in public or parochial education is hard work. I wish that I could say that I've always gladly risen to the occasion, but I've spent enough time crying in my closet and angrily running miles on end to accept that I fail constantly. Eventually, I became so frustrated with myself that I decided I needed a permanent reminder to face whatever was in front of me, big or small.

So, a few years ago I had a new tattoo placed on my arm. I have tattoos that are easily covered by clothing, having gotten my first at sixteen in a tiny shop in Bay City which is now a buffalo wing restaurant. This was going to be my first one that would potentially be visible during the work day and probably something I should not have done on a whim. My husband chalked it up to an early midlife crisis but I felt very strongly that it was the right thing to do. It's a simple script on my inner arm, nothing fancy but large enough to catch attention, and reads "For such a time as this." It's my favorite verse from the book of Esther.

The very bare bones of the story told in the Old Testament is that Esther was a beautiful young girl who was chosen by King Xerxes as a wife, even though she was secretly Jewish. Around the same time an advisor to the king named Haman set about a plan to have all of the Jews put to death due to events perhaps most easily summed up as the Napoleon Complex. Esther's cousin, Mordecai, a less important advisor to the king and himself Jewish, catches wind of this and tells Esther that she needs to approach the king and convince him to change his mind. She is understandably hesitant because appearing in the king's court without invitation is punishable by death, even for the queen, and also there was the whole issue of being secretly Jewish. Esther's cousin, Mordecai, proceeds to give her what is basically the greatest Biblical buttkicking ever recorded, culminating in verse 4:14 "And who knows but that you have come to your royal position for such a time as this?" Esther is convicted to screw up her courage and goes to the king, he listens, and the evil man who was plotting against the Jews is put to death on the very gallows he had constructed for his genocide.

Of course, there is much much more to this story, and we will get to all of that. Esther 4:14 is a good place to start.

For such a time as this. Even prior to the hellish start of the 2017 school year, I felt an affinity to this verse. I have loved having it placed on my arm where it serves as a daily reminder to me that I have been blessed, challenged, loved, hated, strengthened, and supported at various times in my life, all of which has prepared me for each moment God calls me to face and that I do not face those moments alone. It reminds me that my strength does not come from myself or from those around me, but only from God. It also gives me the buttkicking that I sometimes need when I find myself dragging my feet and hoping that situations will resolve without my involvement. As we trudged through the aftermath of 1 October this verse repeatedly popped up, whether it was emailed to us by parents, quoted in devotions, or written in cards of encouragement.

The litter was finally born November 12 and the kennel owner sent out adorable pictures of fuzzy orange chunk nugget puppies chugging around their momma. The mother dog had the same shell shocked look of all first time mothers, peering at the camera with the standard look of panic and exhaustion. Each picture posted lifted my heart and I began sharing them with my students. I was pinning up a few of the cutest ones to the bulletin board outside of my office when my CEO, Steve, passed by and shuddered.

"Ugh," he visibly recoiled. "Cujos. That is a pile of killers right there. What are you going to name our little Cujo? I was thinking we could call her Faith."

"Esther." Dan and I had been discussing this for a while.

"Ah, Esther. I can't argue with that." He continued to his meetings while I went on looking at the pile of puppies and wondering which one would eventually become our Esther and join us in trying to help these kids.

A short while later I found myself back in my CEO's office writing up the strangest document of my career; a working contract/custody agreement/will hashing out how the school and my family will handle details of the dog. I felt strongly that I wanted to personally purchase and own Esther as I struggle with the notion of an organization, even one as amazing as my school, owning an animal. If the program were to not go as planned, if

Esther was to turn out to be untrainable, if any number of things happened, I wanted it to be clearly laid out that Esther would get an early retirement and be able to come home with me and just be a dog. Equally I wanted to make sure that the school was vested in the program and that I wasn't creating a situation where I brought my personal pet to school every day. We laid out the financial details of what the school would contribute; a minimal amount but enough to have a stake in success.

Then it got a little weirder. I hadn't even laid eyes on the puppies in real life yet, but I wanted to figure out solutions to potential issues before any of us were staring an adorable puppy in the adorable puppy eyes.

"What if you fire me?" I asked Steve.

"What if you quit?" he countered.

"No, seriously. Where am I going to go? We are in Vegas for the long haul. What if you fire me one day? Who gets the dog? Could you potentially fire me AND take my dog all in one day?"

We silently stared at each other across his desk. Finally, he chuckled.

"Courtney. You're beloved around here. I think you would have to punch a kid before we would fire you."

I'd be lying if I didn't admit that at several points over two decades in education I had indeed considered punching a kid, albeit fleetingly. Equally it was good to know where the bar for my continued employment was set.

"I appreciate that. But no one plans to get divorced and no one plans to get fired and I think we need to figure out what will happen to the dog if I get fired."

We finally agreed that if I was let go within the first five years of the dog's program, I would pay back the amount the school had contributed and retain ownership of the dog.

"What if one day Zack wakes up and decides he hates the dog and he can't do this anymore?" Steve worried.

"I think of all the things I've made Zack deal with, the dog is pretty harmless."

"No. I can't imagine having one of these things in the house. What if he can't take it one day? Where does the dog go?"

I do love the fact that the idea of having a dog in the house is so foreign to Steve that he imagines it is a burden that will cause a person to snap one day. Like we are taking a needy exotic animal into our home and subjecting our family to relentless around the clock care and also a life of danger.

"Oh, man. What if I die? What if I die and my kids have to deal with the loss of me and now what about their dog? What if the school takes the dog?"

"I'm not going to take the dog away from the kids after your funeral! Who would do that?"

"I DON'T KNOW! But what if you aren't in charge anymore and someone else is and they have it out for me and I go and die and then what?"

We worked through the resolution of as many hypothetical situations as we could imagine. I am now willing to admit that there is a very slim possibility that I escalated a bit more than necessary. However, I do think it is important to have solutions to problems before emotions get involved, even during the very best of times. During this period of time emotions were riding so high and anxiety about everything was heightened.

I don't know that Steve was as concerned about all of these things as I was, being that he was more inclined to be comfortable giving the dog away at any point but I was so anxious about how this would work out and how to lay it all out correctly. I think even then, before any of the craziness started, I knew that this was going to be a big deal and I wanted to take care of all of the details. Not many CEOs would be willing to kill an afternoon discussing the details of a puppy custody agreement, but I am so grateful to Steve for humoring me. I think no one was more surprised than Steve when he found himself interviewing the new puppy for her job a few months later, in what has become one of her most iconic pictures. In the meantime, we just continued the countdown until Esther came home.

Chapter 3

Sidebar: It's Business Time

The Nitty Gritty of Laying Out a Facility Dog Program

IF YOU'VE PICKED UP this book because you want to learn more about the book of Esther, you just enjoy cute dog pictures, or you know me personally and felt guilted into a purchase: feel free to skip ahead to chapter 4.

If you are interested in beginning a canine program in your own school or business and are curious about what the road from puppyhood to working dog looked like, this chapter is going to be your jam.

As you begin to formulate what this kind of program would look like for you, I ask that you remember two things. First, while it's important that all parties involved enter into this in full agreement, before the adorable puppy arrives, it's equally important to realize that much of this is just going to develop organically. The dog will fill holes in your program that you didn't realize even existed, but may also fail to achieve what you hoped in other areas. It's perfectly normal to allow things to evolve and find a rhythm. Second, whenever I speak to anyone about embarking on this journey, I plead with them to remember to just relax. The first two years of this work is going to feel like trying to get through church with a toddler while simultaneously doing your job every day. I remember feeling like I was under a microscope and there were mysterious people in the wings just looking for small failures every day. It took a long time to realize that I actually had a supportive cheering section.

Either way, take a breath and remember to relax.

The custody agreement wasn't the only forward planning that we did, and I began to compile a list of what we did right. It was surprising to me that in the first year of Esther's work she received a lot of publicity, which resulted in a number of educators from around the country reaching out for that advice on how to copy the program. I'm always delighted to get these calls, because I really do believe that every child should have the opportunity to pet a dog when they are struggling. It is magical and I've seen it work so many times. My best concrete advice to those in the very early stages of planning a program is to determine three key areas before even laying eyes on a puppy.

First, figure out what you want your program to look like. Is this going to be primarily outreach work or do you want a dog to serve your population solely? The good folks at Lutheran Church Charities do amazing work with their dogs. Congregations purchase the dogs, fully trained, and the dogs work in the church and around the community. The program creates unique opportunities for a ministry to extend its reach far beyond its walls. When a crisis arises, the dogs and handlers are dispatched to the scene. This is what happened for us on October 3rd, dogs flew in from all over the country to help our kids. I am forever grateful to these heroes and the work that they do.

I thought long and hard about incorporating an LCC Comfort Dog into our school. The pros were huge: the dog would arrive fully trained, it was a system that was proven to work, it would give us an opportunity to further impact the community around us, and it would broaden our mission field nationwide. It all sounded great, but when I really considered both my vision and what our actual needs were, this wasn't the program for us. I knew that I had 2,000 kids on my campus every day and that those kids on any given day were facing a good deal of trauma. Close family members passed away, cancer diagnoses were given, parents divorced, families fell apart. It made me nervous to think that we could have our dog out caring for another community when she was needed at home.

Perhaps a little bit more trivial was the issue of shedding and allergies. As mentioned, two members of our administrative team are highly allergic to dogs and LCC exclusively uses adorable fluffy golden retrievers. Already owning a 200lb tan colored shedding machine, I considered a life in which I could never wear black pants again. One where my desk was full of lint rollers, and two of my dearest colleagues could no longer come to my office. This was what landed us on a Goldendoodle, over my husband's protests that they were the "ugliest dogs" he's "ever seen." It's worth noting his tune changed when we brought home what appeared to be a living Fozzie Bear. It's also worth noting that while no dog is 100% hypoallergenic, I have repeatedly rubbed Esther on all of my allergic coworkers and all parties involved managed to survive it quite nicely.

To be painfully honest, I felt selfish in this decision to keep our dog at Faith and not out in the mission field. The great commission is pretty clear, we are to go and make disciples of all nations. We know that God commands us to serve others and care for the poor; both the physically poor and the poor in spirit. I spent a number of sleepless nights stewing that I was failing to help Faith fulfill a grand call. Even worse, I felt guilty. Our school is in a very affluent area of Las Vegas. To be fair, we have more kids receiving financial aid than not and most families make sacrifices to have their children attend there. That said, I do not have kids who worry where their next meal is coming from or who face any horrors of poverty. There are some days that feel like my job exists to bless the blessed. That can feel disheartening. My school is led by creative visionaries who are geniuses at expanding and moving forward to provide great opportunities. Our campus looks like a small college and boasts three gyms, a courthouse, a working greenhouse, a television production studio, two robotics labs, a molecular genetics lab (I don't actually know what is in that room or how it works), and a 900 seat performing arts center. Our students could experience things that were far out of reach for most. I had moments where I second guessed myself; was I just buying a puppy for a school full of kids who already had been given everything they ever wanted?

Every hard day in my office dispelled that. While money can provide a nice cushion for safe living, the reality is that it does not protect kids from all of the hard things in life. Trauma and tragedy are the great equalizers. While my kids may not want for food, sadly many of them are no strangers to the fear that comes along with domestic abuse. Money does not protect us from illness, from accidents, from tragedies. My wealthiest families still had to bury their own. There are still calls that have to be placed to protective services. I've worked in very poor schools before and I do not want to minimize the challenges they face. I know firsthand that in so many ways it is far easier to be the one organizing the clothing drive rather than the one hoping shoes that fit would be donated to the little ones in my class. But watching these terrified girls cry as they described trying to survive the shooting and mourning with a boy who just lost his mother left me resolved that our kids deserved any extra measure of help I could provide. I resolved that our dog would stay on our campus exclusively to be prepared to help our kids at any time.

Second, it's important to figure out a loose design of the program while understanding that the program will continue to evolve after the arrival of the dog. I wanted to avoid a situation where I just brought my personal dog to work every day. She would need to be more a part of campus life than just hanging out in my office. We figured out ways that she would be plugged in once she was fully trained. One area that I targeted was our Mark 10:14 program, which serves students with a variety of intellectual and developmental ability levels. It is a beautiful program that makes sure all of its students are fully incorporated in daily life around campus. The Mark 10 students are more than included in life at Faith, they are rock stars. Our general education students are delighted when they learn they have a Mark 10 student in their class. I talked with the director of the program to see where Esther could be beneficial. We also worked to roughly outline a way that teachers could "check her out" and have her come be in the classroom on request. I hoped it would work. The nice thing about all of this forward planning was that it really helped everyone to buy in and be excited about the dog.

In another vein, it's important to decide up front where responsibility for the dog will land. Owner versus handler is really the greatest question; will the dog be owned by the organization and live with a variety of trained handlers or will the dog be privately owned and contracted to work? There are certainly pros and cons to both models. Having a series of handlers keeps the dog fresh and exposes it to different people and situations, as well as allowing a larger group of stakeholders to be involved in the day to day of the dog program. The LCC program is set up to work this way and it is an extremely successful model.

We went the private owner route, partly because there were just already so many variables at play and adding a rotation of handlers felt insurmountable. I wanted the dog to always have a soft place to land and to live as close to a normal dog life as possible. It makes things much less complicated as far as scheduling the dog to work and to go to training. It does mean that the financial responsibility for medical, grooming, and upkeep lands squarely on my family. While determining ownership seems simple, there is a lot to be said for having it all figured out before staring at a large vet bill!

Probably the best thing we did came on the recommendation of another professional. Before Steve agreed to the dog, back in my lobbying days, I made contact with Dave Enters. Dave is a fantastic human being who works as a counselor at Concordia University, Wisconsin, home to Zoey the Comfort Dog. Zoey lives on the campus working with a variety of student handlers. She has had such an impact on the university student body that they began fundraising for more dogs in only her second year of working there. Four years after Zoey's arrival, Sage the Comfort Dog began her work with the school's Occupational Therapy and Physical Therapy students, training them to use dogs in their work once they are out in the field. The success of this program has led Concordia to begin fundraising for a third dog, who will eventually work in the school of education. The ways that this university trailblazes these programs is inspiring. Zoey, who is something of an OG of Comfort Dogs, does her serious work in the counseling office, but is also available for students who simply find themselves missing the family pet and needing a dog to love.

My initial conversations with Dave were about finding data to sway Steve over to my side of the dog debate and he delivered. He spoke about Zoey being such a part of campus life that whenever they had a student suffer a loss the students knew to request Zoey upon returning to campus. Dave also spoke with me about the calm Zoey brings to therapy sessions, particularly when working with abuse survivors. In the counseling world, we know that it can take many sessions before the client feels comfortable enough to open up about acute traumatic incidents. Mr. Enters had this to say about one particular student:

> As you can imagine it was a tremendous surprise to me when a young woman who was sexually assaulted opened up to me about her traumatic event in the second session that we met. She was a student who had come to know and love Zoey, our Comfort Dog, from interacting with her around campus. She requested that Zoey join us for our counseling appointments. It is hard to describe the impact that Zoey had with her but it was not hard to observe her impact. While she was petting Zoey she began to talk about what happened. At first I was caught off guard. I was expecting our time to be focused on developing trust and rapport, but she began talking as if that was already in place. It is as if being with Zoey gave her a sense of confidence or courage or a sense of security and/or assurance that it was going to be OK to share her story. It was truly amazing to see. And I have seen Zoe's astonishing influence play out in other counseling relationships that I have had. (Zoey) lifts their spirits, improves their mood, and makes their day."

Now that I had the green light from Steve with the help of all of this data, I turned to Dave again for some guidance. To again be totally and painfully transparent, I had put up such a good front that I knew what I was doing and everything was going to be fine and now that there was a dog on the way and all eyes were on me I was getting more than a little concerned that I was in over my head. Once again, Dave had all of the good advice for me, advice so good that I've passed it on to anyone who has casually asked me about starting up a dog program.

Most importantly, he advised me to control the messaging to our community about the dog right out of the gate. My mission was to get everyone excited and bought into the idea of the dog, while gently reminding them that the dog did not mean that Faith was suddenly a dog friendly campus. I'll admit, I laughed at little at that when he glossed over it in our first conversation. I didn't imagine that starting a canine program could be seen as an invitation for open season with pets at school. It seems like such a simple idea, but it was amazing how many people thought that the arrival of the Comfort Dog meant that they could bring their own dogs onto campus.

Even before we announced the dog, once word got out that the LCC dogs had been at school, I had an alarming number of stay at home moms turn up in my office midday with a fluffy ball in their arms.

"I saw you had the Comfort Dogs here. This is (insert oddly human name). He's nice. I thought I could take him to the cafeteria and the kids could pet him."

It was surprising to me how often I had to explain the difference between the family pet and a trained Comfort Dog.

And why family pets aren't allowed in the cafeteria.

And just how difficult it can be to navigate moms and dogs back out to the parking lot.

But it did reinforce just how nice it is to pet a dog during the school day.

We also had to be proactive in the messaging about why we were getting the dog. In a harshly politicized world where liberals think the conservatives are inhumanely harsh and the conservatives think the liberals are too soft to survive, we've really lost the ability to just accept that sometimes we can do things to make tragedy hurt less and that it is more than acceptable to pursue those things. We were careful to remind our stakeholders that we hadn't forgotten the importance of resilience, we believe in kids working to overcome obstacles, and we do not shield our students from challenges or support parents in snowplowing an easy path for them. We included the following excerpt in a blog post about Esther:

> We believe in student resiliency at Faith Lutheran Middle School & High School. The idea of raising "snowflakes" or children who cannot cope with life's realities is a hotly debated issue in the worlds of parenting, politics, and education. We do not believe that Esther is an unnecessary fluffy (literally) crutch for children to use to avoid life. The unfortunate truth is that many students do experience trauma. Even without the horror

of 1 October, students deal with death, sickness, abuse, anxiety, and very real hurt.

While we hope that none of our students will face hard issues, it gives me comfort to know that the kids will already know Esther and know that she is available when circumstances arise. On calm and peaceful days, Esther will still bring joy to campus.

It was also surprising to me that I had zero negative response to the advent of this program. Not a single parent called to voice concerns. I didn't hear a contradictory peep from anyone on campus, which either means that everyone bought in or that they were just kind enough to not bring their negativity to me. Most plausible is that it was such a hard year at our school that everyone was just so desperate for some good news. I have heard the same sentiments from others who have followed in creating Comfort Dog programs. The pros continue to outweigh the cons and the success stories are heartwarming. If you are looking to start your own program, stay the course and don't give up!

Chapter 4

An Unexpected Queen

ESTHER'S HOME KENNEL, 4E, is just so top notch. At days old the puppies begin a regime of testing to see what their temperament is and if they might be suited to be working dogs. The babies are exposed to different scents to see who shows aptitude to potentially work as diabetic or seizure alert dogs. They are poked and prodded to see who might grow up with the need to both please and be touched, which is so necessary in a therapy dog. They are placed in stressful situations and given puzzles to solve, to see who might be able to work as a service dog and solve problems for an owner. Nursery staff take careful notes of how the puppies react to each new challenge and begin to create aptitude profiles.

Because it is uncertain until going home time what the temperament will most likely be, no one knows until the day the puppies are picked up which dog they will be getting. I was first on the list to pick from the litter and the kennel owner told me that while she would give me the results of the testing, she would not mandate which dog to take. For this kind of work we would have to look for a tolerant and intelligent dog, who genuinely enjoyed the company of people and wanted to be with them at all times. Armed with only this knowledge, my family and I eagerly gazed at the new puppy pictures as the kennel posted them and waited impatiently for visitation day.

My dear friend, Jill Heupel, is a remarkably talented photographer and the brilliant lens behind all of the pictures in this book. What is so mind blowing about Jill is that she can take pictures of families, food, dogs, and newborn babies and have all subjects turn out looking gorgeous. For years she has been creating enviable portraits of my very ordinary family. She also loves dogs as much as I do. When I told her that we were finally going to get a dog for the school she volunteered her services as the official photographer of the comfort dog.

For real. Our newborn puppy was going to have professional paparazzi.

One Saturday in December, the kennel had visitation day for the litter. We got to meet the parents of our future puppy and play with the sweet babies. They all had fox names, because their sweet mother Cybil looks like a little fox. Jill came along, with some very expensive camera equipment, and everyone tried to act like it was normal for formal pictures of six week old puppies to be happening. Because the kennel is legit, there was a serious sanitizing process before going inside; soaking shoes, wearing booties, alcohol wipes, the whole nine yards. Eventually Jill, my daughter, and I made our way into the large room where the puppies were waiting.

I am convinced that heaven will look like a large room where there are puppies waiting.

My daughter, Petey, dove right into the pile and the little furry tanks began clambering right over her. One, wearing an orange ribbon and going by the name of Arctic, was particularly adorable. She was tiny and had a white burst of fur on her orange chest. She let Petey carry her all over and kept falling asleep while being held. I watched her snuggle her sweet face into Petey's shoulder while she ignored both the stream of commentary coming from Petey and the way she was being bounced around.

"I bet that one winds up being our dog." I told Jill.

Jill agreed and most of the pictures she snapped that day were of sweet Arctic. She took some of the other puppies as well. The only one she didn't get was the one wearing a red ribbon and going by Eevee. I didn't consider Eevee for a second, because she was a square dinosaur of a puppy who never stopped moving. While the other puppies would frequently tip over and succumb to adorable puppy snores, this one waddled over all the obstacles in front of her whether they were toys or humans. Eevee chewed on the tails of siblings and gave little growls as she tugged on the clothing of visitors. She was exhausting and I chuckled to myself thinking about the poor family stuck with a nonstop Frank the Tank puppy.

After we pet all of the puppies and kissed quite a few on their mouths, Jill dragged Petey and I out of there. We stopped at a tiny Mexican restaurant on the way home and mulled over which puppy might eventually be ours. We unanimously agreed that it would probably be sweet Arctic. My son had missed the fun of the day due to practice and we called him on the way home.

"I think we've figured out which one it will be!" I was so excited to tell him and sad that he had missed the events of the day.

"Eevee." He had spent the last hour looking at pictures of the puppies online and had his own guess ready.

"No way. That puppy was crazy. I can't imagine her being a Comfort Dog."

"Nope. It's Eevee. I bet you."

He still can't explain why he was so certain and I can't explain why I didn't take that bet.

And so the waiting period began. We bought crates, baby gates, tiny sweaters, and the shampoo and conditioner that the kennel recommended for the prone to dreadlock Goldendoodle hair. Daily we checked for updated pictures on the kennel's Instagram page.

"It'll be Eevee." My son remained stoic in his prediction, no matter how much my daughter and I howled at him that he was wrong. My husband looked forward to getting on with it, although he claimed that I had repressed just how stressful having a puppy really is.

Eventually the kennel released the evaluation videos of the puppies. Every puppy had a few moments on film with the owner's young daughter. They had the chance to come when called and were picked up and had their tails gently tugged to see how they reacted to the stress. We eagerly watched all of the videos. When Eevee's came up we saw the young girl pick up a round puppy with a fat belly. She tugged on the puppy's tail and the puppy responded by trying to kiss her on the mouth.

"NO, Eevee!" The girl spit out the kiss.

"Oh, Eevee. . . . .did you get denied again?" We could hear Jeannette, the kennel owner, laughing off camera, as Eevee stared mournfully at the camera.

Later that night, we received summaries of the aptitude and temperament testing for each dog. Eevee was off the charts with a drive to please, intelligence, and a need to be touched.

Hesitantly, I emailed Jeannette to ask if Eevee was clearly the pick to become our Esther. She replied that she wouldn't tell me which dog to take but that yes, it would be the most logical choice for our therapy dog.

Eevee. The dog of nap refusal and sibling tail chewing. The one who never seemed to quite settle down.

My son could not stop carrying on about being right. We spent the rest of the evening going back through all of the pictures posted since birth and paying special attention to the little fat one with the red ribbon. She seemed oddly unstoppable. In every picture she was wide awake, badgering siblings and climbing all over the momma dog.

"We probably should buy a few more gates." Zack mused as he looked over our shoulders at a picture of young Eevee charging through the water dishes.

I think it was about that time that I began to really relate to this dog, however weird that might sound. For a church worker, my past is not very . . . church worker. I went to Lutheran school from Kindergarten to 8th grade, but my home life and my story are very different from the down home Midwestern upbringings of my coworkers. My dad was most certainly not a pastor and my parents have not been married for half a century. They actually have six marriages between the two of them and my siblings are numerous steps and halfs some of whom I've never even met. Addiction holds hands and skips along with depression and anxiety through both sides of my family trees.

I sometimes struggle to relate to the warm and fuzzy stories my co-workers share and I certainly struggle when the holiday season rolls around and they head home to large extended family Christmases, while I stay here with my kids and pray that my husband doesn't get called out again leaving us to celebrate just the three of us.

Aside from my family dynamic, which is admittedly out of my control, I didn't always do a good job of taking care of the things that were under my control and oftentimes verged even further from my coworkers in my life choices. Zack and I lived together before we were married. I lost a lot of time over the years to drinking more wine than I should and allowing low level anxiety to paralyze me into total inaction. I've been known to cuss like a sailor, something I am still working on. I got into all sorts of trouble in high school and made some pretty questionable choices in college as well.

And so sometimes, as I look around at my polished colleagues, I can't help but think "Are you SURE, God?"

Are you sure about me? Me being the one to witness for you and me being the one that kids might accidentally use as a standard of Christian living? What if my past haunts me? What if I am found out? Does that make me a fake? And does that do even more damage to the kingdom of heaven?

The problem with that kind of thinking is that it brings a whole lot of shame along with it. Guilt is the feeling that we did something wrong, while shame is the feeling that we are something wrong. Shame says that we are different, dirty, unlovable. The worst part about shame is that it not only makes us feel ashamed but that it also can make us act out to overcompen-sate and try to hide our insecurities. It is odd how hard it is for shame and humility to coexist.

As I watched this seemingly out of control puppy maul her siblings and refuse to nap, I related. Here we both were, getting called into a ministry that seemed to have chosen us. Seemingly ill equipped, unprepared and possibly not up for the job.

And all of this reminded me of dear Queen Esther, the puppy's namesake.

The opening chapter of the book of Esther begins with King Xerxes in a bit of a bind. It's 483 B.C. and this king is down to party. Xerxes is the 5th king of Persia. He is proud, impulsive, and fond of hosting giant banquets. Here we find him 180 days in to what is basically a party meant to display the wealth of his kingdom and his prowess as a leader. In the midst of this revelry, he summons his wife, Vashti, so that he could display her beauty. Tired of his shenanigans and prepared to make a bold political move of her own, she refused. Which placed him in the awkward and emasculated position of believing he risked a rebellion of all of the females in his land or drawing a hard line in the sand.

He drew the hard line in the sand and had her deposed as Queen.

Perhaps a more introspective man would have been saddened over the loss of the woman he reportedly adored. Our man Xerxes chooses to basically hold a reality show style competition to see who should be the next queen. And here we find the lovely Esther, the adopted niece of Mordecai, who serves as one of the King's advisors. They both also happened to be Jewish.

All of this is taking place about 100 years after the exile of the Jews. While Jews were gaining some traction in Persia, beginning to own their own businesses and even holding positions in government, they were still outsiders.

Outsiders. Less thans. The kind of people who could be in respected positions as long as they weren't too vocal, didn't rock the boat, and kept their sheer "Jewishness" quiet.

In this climate, Esther entered into the pageant seeking the king's affection. She was, by all accounts, not only beautiful but also charismatic and engaging. Her guardian, Mordecai, instructed her to stay silent about being Jewish. While Mordecai, as a Jew, had been placed in the role of advisor to the King he still did not trust that a Jewish woman would be received as Queen. What an odd place for Queen Esther to land. She had the knowledge that she had been selected for a very important position, but secret shame that she wasn't "good enough" for the job.

I've realized over the course of a few years, being utterly imperfect me trying to keep the plates of my normal job duties spinning and also learning to counsel and care for seriously traumatized individuals while hauling a puppy along for the ride, that I am so grateful for my own murky past because it makes me relatable. The same way the children are delighted and endeared when a bark slips out of Esther or she has an accident in the choir hallway (ONE TIME), I become humbled and relatable when I own my past and use the experience for connection. It is so much healthier than hiding it away, being ashamed, and hoping to not be found out. I am an imperfect sinful person, struggling every single day to help imperfect sinful people. I understand the pain of poor decisions and the guilt of turning my back on what I know to be right. I also painfully understand the feeling of being less than, or not good enough for the role you find yourself placed in.

My friends, in all aspects of the ministry and life, we are fearfully and wonderfully made. God calls us into his work, warts and all, because it is a battle we are able to fight with Him. We will never know how revealing our vulnerabilities will help someone else to heal. For such a time as this, indeed.

Even with knowing God called me to this job, stepping into administration brought a whole new level of anxiety for me, which pooled eagerly with my existing generalized anxiety. Is there a worse feeling than surveying a situation and thinking that someone should really do something about it and then realizing that you are the someone that should actually be doing something? What happens when you are supposed to be the adultiest adult in the room? I am not really wired to be a buck stops here kind of person, as I prefer being the affirmer to everyone and just kind of soothing things along.

We can all find reasons to step aside and let someone else handle things. But what if, what IF, the battle in front of you right now is one that you were meant to fight? Even though it may be long and hard and you may feel ill equipped, what if it was the very reason you were created? These moments when God taps us on the shoulder and calls us to action are so uncomfortable, especially when we are already struggling with shame, guilt, and pain. Finding the quiet is so important in these times, the long walks, silent bubble baths, moments stolen without distraction. In the silence we find direction and in God's direction we find strength. Pressing into battle might look like a fuzzy orange dog or it might look like confronting an injustice, dealing with a toxic relationship, or helping someone else in need. Look for strength in the uncomfortable.

Chapter 5

There is No Such Thing as Coincidence

It ALWAYS AMAZES ME how doors will often fly open when you are proceeding down a path that is God's plan for you. There will still be work and stress, but things will fall into place in a supernatural way. The book of Esther appears, at first glance, to be a series of coincidences that culminate in a breathless grand finale. The reality is that the apparently absent God is snapping piece after piece of groundwork into place for His plan.

My favorite "coincidence" in the book of Esther involves an uncovered murder plot and a sleepless night. A foiled murder plot? I told you this book was one great big soap opera.

Shortly after Esther is named Queen, Mordecai is out one day just minding his own business at the gates of the city. He happens to overhear two of King Xerxes' guards hatching a plan to kill him. Mordecai reports this to his cousin, the new Queen Esther, who repeats it to the King, making sure to give the credit for the discovery to Mordecai. This speaks to Esther's character, that she is willing to pass along the props for such a big discovery. Xerxes investigates the accusation, discovers it to be true, has the two guards hanged, and this little bit of history is recorded in the royal records.

And so time marched on in the city of Susa. I have to believe threats to murder the king were fairly commonplace and people were hung for lesser grievances. This foiled murder plot should have been a tiny blurb in the story of the city, something that no one would have ever expected to have greater implications. Meanwhile, Esther stays Queen and a man named Haman is promoted to the rank of highest official to the king. Intoxicated with his newfound power, Haman decreed that all of the city officials had to bow to him at the city gates. Being Jewish and sworn to only bow to God, Mordecai refused to bend the knee to Haman.

This did not go over well with Haman. The Bible does not give a physical description of Haman but it is easy to imagine him as a small angry man, red faced and pounding desks when things don't go his way. He decided to take holding a grudge to an entirely new level, vowing to not only murder Mordecai but to put an end to the entire Jewish community throughout the kingdom.

I guess it's possible that genocide plots have hatched over lesser slights? It's hard to imagine, though. Haman gets in the king's ear about a group of people out to get to him. Xerxes, either entirely checked out or just worn down by repeated reports of people meaning him harm, agrees that Haman can carry out his plot and start building gallows. Esther 3:15b probably best sums up what it must have been like to live under the reign of King Xerxes:

"The king and Haman sat down to drink, but the city of Susa was bewildered."

Then one night King Xerxes couldn't sleep. Coincidentally, this sleeplessness happened the night of Esther's first banquet, which was also the night before Haman planned to request Mordecai's execution. Now, a lot of things happened between the night the king first agreed to murder the Jews and this particular sleepless night, but it is so important to clearly draw the connection of Mordecai's grand coincidence. He did not just causally overhear a murder plot, it turns out. The entire book paints Xerxes as kind of a drunken oaf and so I imagine his night was like any night in middle age when too much wine has been consumed and there is that rebound wake up around 2am as the last bits of alcohol are metabolizing. In modern times, it's when we lay awake and roll around in our anxiety until we either drift back off or get up for the day.

Or is that just me?

Xerxes had the luxury of servants at his beck and call, so rather than languishing in anxiety and dehydration he called a few in and asked to have the royal records read back to him. This is yet another interesting coincidence. The royal records? This is the King we are talking about and his means for diverting his attention from sleepless anxiety were actually endless. He could have had wives or concubines brought to him, requested a soothing music concert be played in his rooms, or dragged in court performers for jokes and tricks. Instead he requested that the royal records be read to him. The royal chronicles were painstaking day by day accounts of the things that happened to the king. Where he went, what he ate, if anything interesting happened that day involving other people.

To be clear, this would be like waking up anxious and deciding that instead of Netflix or a good book to lull you back to sleep, you would like to review your tax records.

The servant read the royal chronicles until morning, peaking the King's interest when he got to the part about Mordecai foiling a murder plot. Xerxes realized in the retelling that Mordecai had never been rewarded for this act. This seems a little crazy, to have someone intervene on a murder conspiracy and not even get a thank you, but I highly doubt Xerxes was a thank you card kind of guy.

Rising from bed, Xerxes runs into Haman and casually asks him what would be a good reward for invaluable service. Assuming the king is referring to him, Haman is overly enthusiastic about being paraded about town on a horse in fine robes while people cheer.

Who wouldn't want that? And how mad was Haman a few hours later as he not only watched Mordecai get paraded about the city but had to be one on foot leading his horse? Even worse for Haman, he was forced to call everyone's attention to Mordecai, the man the king chose to honor, as they walked.

You know the person who gets under your skin? We all have one, it's ok, this is a safe place to admit it. And while we (hopefully) are never consumed enough by our irritation to plot a hanging, I think that all of us would struggle with having to parade a nemesis about our hometowns while literally singing their praises for all to hear.

It's all so dramatic, which is partly why the book of Esther has long been one of my favorites. Murderous eunuchs, overheard whispers, jockeying for favor with a king, parades about the city, and climactic reveals? Yes, please. It has all of the makings of a hit soap opera. Stepping back from the drama of it all, the heart of this God created coincidence is so relatable. Mordecai is in the right place, at the right time, and hears something that changes the course of his life.

I just love when coincidences begin to stack up and God's gentle whispers become apparent. While less dramatic than foiling a genocide plot, finding Esther's kennel and winding up with Esther herself came about through a series of coincidences. Getting the mail one day in 2016, back when I was still idly hassling my administration about bringing a dog on board, I spotted a new neighbor attempting to leash train what appeared to be an unruly cream colored Muppet. Murphy, as I learned was his name, was a new puppy for some empty nesters. Murphy's 60lbs of unbridled joy hit me in my solar plexus as I asked about where he came from.

"4E Kennels" Murphy's new mom shouted over her shoulder as he dragged her up the street.

A few weeks later I was out for a run and came upon an adorable fluffy orange mop enjoying a walk. Again, a 4E pup. It really sank in when a former student posted her new curly 4E puppy on social media.

I ran into these dogs, all from the same kennel, with increasing regularity. There are a lot of Goldendoodle breeders around Las Vegas, some reputable and some not. After I brought Esther home I would hear about other breeders when I took her for walks or had her in public and people would want to share about the Doodle they had at home. But in the time leading up to purchasing a dog, the only kennel name I ever heard was 4E. God could not have been more clear in guiding me toward that particular breeder. Visiting the 4E website I found Diana, the slightly older pup they were on the fence about rehoming. My reaching out was a little half -hearted, the kennel's waffling about selling her not nearly as frustrating to me as they thought it was. But the perception that I was frustrated from those weeks of back and forth led to a pick of the litter, which led to Esther.

Chapter 6

Bringing Home the Beans

BACK ON CAMPUS, 2017 was mercifully winding down as we ticked toward Christmas vacation. Christmas at Faith Lutheran is my favorite time of year, the campus is beautiful and music pours from all over. Our advent chapels build excitement and even our most skeptical students get caught up in the magic. It is joyful to work in a place where we can prepare for the birth of our Savior so openly and excitedly. My girls from the concert were in often to talk about Christmas vacation plans and share shopping purchases. Clutching red Starbucks holiday cups, they would tell me about where they were planning to travel and the family they would get to see. More than once they individually referenced their excitement over a new year and a fresh start. I tried to match their enthusiasm, but my heart was sinking. Coming through a trauma and falling into the mindset that a specific day would be a new start can be a very dangerous thing. It always makes me nervous when people identify a specific date when "everything will change" or buy into the whole "new year, new me" way of thinking. Inevitably the big day arrives and we are still the same people we were the night before, with the same problems and the same surroundings, which can be devastating when hope was pinned on change. Positive change takes time, healing takes time, and the progress of both is rarely linear.

I did my best to support their holiday spirit while also gently reminding them that we would be back in our daily life right away when school returned in January. They brought gifts for the faculty that had supported them, baked cookies, and showed me pictures of holiday outfits. I prayed that they would find peace and comfort in the Christmas season and maybe even some normalcy as they celebrated with family.

Meanwhile, another trauma was brewing. One of our teachers, Susan, has a twenty-five year old son who had been battling cancer for almost the last two years. Johan, a graduate of Faith Lutheran, lived in Reno with his gorgeous fiancée and frequently traveled to California for treatment. Susan often traveled to be with him, including an extensive surgery over Thanksgiving break which was intended to remove tumors from his lungs. She returned to school from that trip to work the days between Thanksgiving and Christmas break sharing tales of Johan's strength, bravery, and faith. Outspoken and passionate about both his beliefs and the causes he supported, Johan had chosen to have words from Psalm 18 tattooed on his back shortly after arriving at college. After graduation he planned to join the National Guard and later the police academy, looking to continue to find ways to use his gifts to protect and serve others. During the medical evaluations for the National Guard his cancer was discovered. As his health battle raged on, the words from Psalm 18 inked upon his body became even more poignant:

> For who is God besides the Lord?
> And who is the Rock except our God?
> It is God who arms me with strength
> and keeps my way secure.
> He makes my feet like the feet of a deer;
> he causes me to stand on the heights.
> He trains my hands for battle;
> my arms can bend a bow of bronze.

At school the Faith Family continued to pray fervently for miraculous healing for him and for peace and strength for his family. Cancer is ugly and brutal and he had been bravely fighting for some time. This young man taught us all so many lessons in living in gratitude and facing struggles with strength and grace. Susan herself taught us so many lessons about living in the hope of our Lord; we would frequently marvel as a staff about how one of us would attempt to comfort her and would instead wind up being reassured by her. The students and teachers would send letters, cards, posters, and videos to Johan as he both received and recovered from treatment. The students were too young to remember him as student here at Faith, but they loved their teacher so much and wanted to help. Many of the staff had taught Johan in his younger days and would send him teasing notes about his youth. Susan would frequently tell us that the love and support he felt from the teachers and students buoyed him on the hardest of days, but everyone still felt a deep desire to want to do more. We didn't know it at the time, but this holiday season would be Johan's last and he would be in the arms of Jesus by the end of January, fighting bravely until the very end. He left behind a warrior's legacy of humor, faith, hope, and sheer determination that touched not only his huge circle of friends but an entire school community of children who had never met him.

As Christmas break finally arrived, life felt fragile and the holidays seemed more important than ever. I did my best to leave work at work and to focus on my own kids as much as possible, which is impossible when the people I work with are family and I love them so much.

At our house we used the time off to prepare for the arrival of the puppy, as she was coming home two days before I returned to school in January. The week before Evee was to come home and become Esther, another email arrived from the kennel, this one informing us that the puppies had tested positive for giardia. We were advised that the puppies had already started medication, that we could research the treatment plan for this illness, and if we didn't want to deal with it we could move to the waitlist for another puppy.

By this point my children had grown so cyber attached to Eevee that there was no way we could consider this. I set about becoming a giardia expert. Giardia, or beaver fever, is a parasite that dogs can pass back and forth. It's unfortunate, and no reflection on the kennel. A mother dog can carry the virus dormant for most of her life and during the stress of delivery pass it along to the pups. The pups, despite even the most diligent and meticulous efforts, will spend the first two months of their lives mouthing and pooping on each other, gleefully passing the virus around in a way that makes full treatment impossible until they are separated.

The treatment plan seemed manageable. Nightly baths for her little puppy butt with medicated shampoo. Medication sprinkled into her food. Cleaning up after her immediately after she goes to the bathroom. Giardia can cause dog diarrhea, which always carries a risk of dehydration, but appeared to be mostly harmless. I was confident we could handle it.

Zack was less confident.

"Court. We have a two hundred pound mastiff to consider."

This is true. Maeby the mastiff was six years old and really not in a place to be exposed to viruses.

"If that mastiff gets a virus that causes chronic diarrhea and I have to spend the next two months power washing the backyard, I might not recover from it. A man sized dog having bowel explosions all over our turf? Our marriage may actually not recover from it."

Zack's concerns, while upsettingly vivid, were indeed valid. Mastiff diarrhea is not something to be taken lightly. I also hated the thought of potentially putting our gentle giant at risk.

"It'll be ok. We will keep her in puppy jail until there is an all clear. We can do it."

He shook his head and walked off, while I went back to mixing bleach and water in spray bottles. Maeby snored gently in the corner on her giant dog bed, completely unaware that her world was about to get rocked.

The big homecoming day finally arrived and we loaded up to make the hour drive to Pahrump. I believe that in every marriage, there are two kinds of people: one who believes that anything less than a half a tank of gas means you are about to be stranded and one who believes that a quarter tank means that sometime that week you might possibly be stopping to get more. My husband is the latter. It is a source of huge stress because I am always convinced we are about to be left roadside at any moment and he is constantly reminding me that we haven't been stranded yet. This day was no different. We were late leaving for the kennel and when we got in the car we were at a quarter tank of gas.

"It's fine." Zack, still concerned about the potential increase in dog diarrhea we were facing, was in no mood to panic about gas with me. Armed with blankets, dog toys, and plastic bags in case of an accident on the way home the kids bounced up and down in the back seat.

"It's FINE, "they chanted.

I tried to ignore the fact that stress was making the bottoms of my feet sweat and we headed out.

The drive to Pahrump from Vegas is an uneventful stretch of desert, not broken with much to look at. Or gas stations, as it turns out. About twenty miles outside of town the fuel light came on. Sweat poured off of the bottom of my feet. A hush fell over the car while Zack attempted to appear casual in asking me to google where the closest gas station was located. Turns out it was located 14 miles away. We had roughly 14 miles worth of gas left.

I bit my tongue until it bled.

We coasted into the Pahrump gas station on fumes, in a deathly silent car. Zack scurried out to start pumping gas while I texted the kennel owner like a crazy person, convinced that she was going to think that we weren't showing up and give Eevee to another family. She's fine, she's sleeping peacefully waiting for her new family. The sweet woman did her best to console me while I shot Zack the evil eye through the car window and he pretended not to notice.

Eventually we arrived at the kennel, the kids over excited and sticky from the old Halloween candy they had somehow smuggled into the car during the chaos of loading up late. Zack was subdued and still not making eye contact with anyone and I slipped along on my sweaty feet, quietly worrying to myself that I was about to bring a diarrhea ridden hyperactive fluff ball into not only my peaceful home but also my office. An office that was still daily filled with sobbing and traumatized teenagers.

Eevee was indeed sleeping peacefully when we arrived. We went through the entire disinfecting process and made our way into the nursery. Her parents, Cybil and Frankie, joyfully ran the length of the yard, perhaps sensing their impending freedom from the litter of chubby demanding puppies.

The kids scooped her up right away. Startled and disoriented, she immediately began trying to lick their hands and faces, probably partly in affection and partly because they were coated in sugary goodness. Her fat bottom wiggled with delight. We were given the rest of her Giardia medication, instructions on how to follow up with the vet, and a bottle of disinfecting shampoo for her nightly butt baths. The puppy and I regarded each other.

"It'll be ok," her big brown eyes seemed to be saying. "Poop will only rain from the skies for a little while. I'm totally worth it. You're going to love washing my butt every night."

Our going home picture shows all of us gathered around Zack while he holds what appears to be smug and sleepy bear. Once we got Eevee into the car we let her know that her name was now Esther.

"ESTHER. ESTHER. ESTHER." The kids chanted her name in high pitched voices trying to get her attention. Her little head cocked from side to side as she tried to make sense of what was happening. Eventually she gave up and curled back into the blanket supplied by the kennel. Breathing in the scents of her momma and her siblings, she fell back asleep as we journeyed home to Vegas. With a full tank of gas, it should be noted.

Once home, we placed her in her little jail. She sat down and stared curiously around her while the mastiff ventured over to sniff her through the gate. Even Hobbes the cat made an appearance, creeping closer and closer until she let out a high pitched bark that sent him scurrying away to hide in my closet and defile my shoes for the next several days. Mastiff and puppy stared at each other through the bars. Finally, Maeby turned and stared dolefully at me.

"I didn't ask for this," she seemed to be saying. "No one said that I wanted a sister."

I know. I patted her huge cinder block head while the puppy paced in circles around her playpen. The doorbell rang, bringing both Esther's photographer, Jill, and my work husband, Dan.

She perked up to greet Dan and his kids, trotting in circles and letting her fat belly be rubbed. While she was inarguably one adorable puppy, she simply did not stop moving when awake. The kids scooted in circles after her trying to pet her. She was only still when she was sleeping.

Thankfully, after all of that petting the puppy snoozed through the execution of a series newborn pictures that reminded me of the first months of my kids' lives. As infants, they would sleep while I would change them into new adorable outfits, set them back into their bouncy papasan seats, and then snap pictures. I have an entire album of my son in a variety of fancy clothes, all in the exact pose and seat, all sound asleep. Esther squeezed her eyes shut while being forced into a baby bonnet, woke up long enough to look worried while we set her in a box full of feathers, and gently snored while being posed next to several versions of the Faith logo. The pictures turned out so cute that it hurts a little to look at them.

The first month having Esther home screeched by in a blur of bleach water, puppy butt baths, and round the clock trips outside. I've never learned my lesson, so every puppy we have ever owned has come home sometime in December, leaving me standing outside at 2am in my robe during what is the only really cold month of the year in Vegas.

We began to work on walking on a leash, venturing out at 4am to walk around the block with Maeby before I got ready for school. It was dark and cold, scary enough that neither Esther nor I were brave enough to take the walkies without the big dog. I'd put her little pink collar and leash on her and we would stand on the porch together, too afraid to go any farther on our own. Eventually, we would head back in to find Maeby who was also a little less than thrilled. We would walk around the block with Esther pinging back and forth between us. Maeby learned to plod along while Esther repeatedly ricocheted off of the side of her giant head.

Zack would like me to note here that we live in a perfectly safe neighborhood and this is another example of a time that I may have possibly escalated unnecessarily.

Esther did quickly learn to sit on command, leading me to believe that not only was she a puppy genius but that I was a savant dog trainer. We have videos of her tiny bottom hitting the ground when she heard me say sit.

"Seriously," I crowed at Zack "if I could just take like six months off of work I could totally just train her up myself. I don't know why you are so against a sabbatical."

Zack sighed and pointed out that she was sprinting down the hallway with a pair of my underwear. He sighed louder when she refused to come when called and wedged her fat tummy behind the sofa to chew on them in peace.

So, I started looking for a trainer.

Chapter 7

Finding an Adulty-Adult

THE KENNEL GAVE US two recommendations; an organization that did Monday night classes and left a good deal of the training up to the owner as well as an individual who provided dog training services. After an embarrassing amount of time lost to trying to reclaim my underwear from the puppy I was no longer confident in my training abilities. I was hoping to find an adult who could take charge of this situation and started by calling Norton Dog Training. When Brad's booming voice answered his phone, I was hopeful that I had finally found an alpha male to take charge of the sock and underwear theft, the indoor peeing, the 2am barking, and the rapid fleeing at the sound of her name.

I deflated when Brad told me what he charged. I expected a good one on one trainer to be expensive and I knew that Brad's reputation was excellent. I knew that the process of turning a puppy into a working dog was a lengthy one. Still, I was doing most of this out of pocket and also knew that he was out of my budget. I hadn't planned ahead to write grants, raise money, place a line item for dog training into my counseling budget, or any other responsible adult kind of things. I started explaining to him what we were doing and why. I talked about the kids, about how sad campus was every day, and about how I wanted to pioneer a program unlike anything else that was currently out there. I told him the sad stories that I heard all day and the struggle to return to normalcy.

"I can't afford you," I admitted to him. "But this is going to be big and it's going to be public. Do you want to have an adventure with me? Do you think you can cut me a deal?" I paced around my kitchen. On the other end of the line I could hear Brad take a deep breath while I held mine.

"Ok," he finally said. "I'll just do it for free."

I don't know that Brad likes when I tell this part of the story. Later on, he would admit that he hung up the phone shaking his head, unsure of what had just happened. I don't think I was that great of a salesman or that I had him snookered. I think that God placed him in my path at exactly the right time; when his business was picking up but before he was as incredibly in demand as he is these days. More than that, I believe that for all of his booming voice and his take no prisoners presence Brad is one of the most kind hearted and empathetic people I've ever met. That combined with his talent made him the key to our program; he bought in, he genuinely wanted to help others, and he delighted in the ways that Esther changed our campus. It was so clear that all of the publicity that he received in those early years paled in comparison to being involved in such compassionate and important work. I've loved the times that he has come to visit campus and had the chance to see the benefits of his hard work, as kids and adults both light up when they see this goofy orange dog heading down the hallway.

A few days after that awkward phone call he made his first visit to our house to meet us and lay eyes on Esther. He was an imposing figure and his presence matched his voice.

"This is Maeby! Look how well trained she is! She sits and everything! We did that! I can make her lay down! Do you want me to make her lay down? Because I can do that." There was something about him that apparently flared up all of my dormant daddy issues within moments of meeting him and I found myself desperately needing his approval. I also wanted him to know that Zack and I weren't totally hopeless and that we would follow through on what he wanted us to do.

He laughed at me.

"Anybody can train a mastiff. Look at her. She's already back asleep. Let's see how you do with an intelligent high energy Goldendoodle."

I deflated a little. While we were talking, Zack let baby Esther out of her kennel. She bolted toward us, a fuzzy orange streak, and raced around Brad's feet yipping excitedly and stopping only to leave a little puddle of urine on the floor.

"I've been, um, working on that." It wasn't the initial impression I had hoped Esther would make.

Brad scooped her in one arm, laying her little belly along his forearm. "Quiet!" he thundered. The puppy immediately went silent and hung complacently on his arm, staring up at him with the same kind of adoration that I probably had on my face. Brad started calmly talking again like nothing had happened.

What kind of canine witchcraft was this?

"I'm worried about introducing her to campus," I admitted to Brad. "She is so tiny and so cute and I am not sure how to deal with 2,000 kids wanting to meet her."

Brad regarded the tiny hairball snoozing on his arm. "It'll be easier once she doesn't look like a living teddy bear. Plus, working dogs carry themselves differently. You'll see. She won't seem quite to goofy. It'll be ok."

He left us with a short list of things to work on; leash work, sitting, staying, and learning to go to her kennel on command. He also left a longer list of things to buy; collars and leashes, a trampoline bed, fetching toys, and other supplies. Zack and I did our best to seem very confident that we wouldn't let him down. He promised to be in touch shortly and I am almost positive that I saw him shaking his head as he walked back out to his truck. Determined to win his favor, I went straight to Amazon and started filling my cart with the supplies he recommended. Zack hauled the puppy outside to try and convince her that it was more fun to pee on cold turf than warm wooden floors. She peered at him skeptically and then snatched a stick and scooted out of reach under the trampoline to eat it.

Thanks to Amazon Prime the supplies Brad demanded began arriving quickly. We now had an off the ground trampoline style bed where she was supposed to lay when told to place. Instead she discovered how much fun it was to use as a springboard when she chased the mastiff around the house. There was the Mighty Mac collar that had just a few links of chain on it, meant to snap when I needed to her behave on leash. It didn't hurt or frighten her in the least and was incredibly effective in getting some of her pinging around under control on her walks. It also incited blind rage among some members of the dog rescue community when I posted a picture of her wearing it.

"What in the world?" I showed Zack the angry messages I'd received on Esther's Instagram account after posting a picture of her happily posing while on a walk in her new collar.

"I don't get it. She is happy to put it on, isn't afraid of it, hasn't once yipped while wearing it. . .. ." Esther raced by in her new collar, springing from the trampoline platform of her new bed to collide with the muscular wall of her new big sister. "These messages make it seem like I'm burning her with lit cigarettes every time she doesn't sit."

Little did I know that by creating social media accounts for this little monster I was opening myself up to a world of criticism about things I hadn't known existed. Essentially publicly training a puppy to work, while documenting it on the internet, gave a platform for people to rally against every move we made.

We were too firm. Not firm enough. That collar with the rings is inhumane. That collar without the rings is inhumane because it has no give. She needs to be walked more. She needs to be walked less, are you trying to mess up her hips? Have you tried only positive reinforcement? Treats for everything? Stop giving her so many treats. She is getting fat.

Yes, my dog has totally been body shamed on social media.

In the end, I did what any reasonable professional would do. I enlisted my tech savvy teen to get really good at photoshop. Rarely can you see what kind of collar Esther is wearing in her pictures, because I honestly just don't have the strength to care what people think any more. She is a happy, healthy, little dog who rotates between three very different collars and is just as delighted to see each one because each collar means that it is adventure time.

A few days after our first meeting with Brad I tossed Esther into her downstairs kennel and left Petey in charge of babysitting while Zack worked to fill in the holes she had dug in the yard and I took a shower. Approximately fourteen seconds after stepping into the hot water and lathering up, I was interrupted by hysterical shrieking.

"Mom!! Esther just threw up! Esther just threw up a snake!"

A snake? This was new. I'm not sure where the puppy would find a snake to consume and then throw up, but I didn't doubt her tenacity. I galloped wetly down the stairs in my towel to find Zack running in covered in dirt. In these various states of disarray the three of us considered the puppy, who was standing proudly next to something that appeared to be a freshly regurgitated green snake and wagging her tail. I scooped up the puppy while Zack poked at the snake with a pen. We collectively held our breath and waited for the verdict.

"It's a sock. Petey, it's one of your green footie socks."

"Do I get it back?" Petey was concerned. I pressed on the puppy's round belly to see if she was in any kind of discomfort. She wriggled with delight and started licking the soap off of my arm.

"No, you don't get it back. . . . .please go upstairs and make sure you haven't left any socks laying around."

We cleaned out the kennel while Esther snuggled into the mastiff's large stomach. I worried that maybe she had eaten more socks and they hadn't come up yet.

"What if she has a bowel obstruction? What if she dies? Aside from the general horror of a puppy dying, what if I just got an entire sad school community excited about this puppy and then she is killed by socks?"

Zack sighed again. "I guess it's good we have pet insurance. Call the vet and let them know that we are headed in."

A few hundred dollars and hours later, we were in the clear. Esther had an empty stomach, was safe, and was clearly delighted in the attention she received at the vet. She raced around the office greeting everyone with excited kisses. The vet warned us that once dogs eat a sock they are prone to forever eating socks. We shrugged off the warnings and vowed to keep a closer eye on her. Little did we know that this orange fuzzy mess was secretly a dumpster dog, prone to sucking up everything in her path with a quickness that made it impossible to stop her. She was basically a furry Roomba.

Later that day Brad called to check in on our training progress. I may have slightly over exaggerated our success with the basic skills he asked us to work on, but I was proud to report that she could make it to the end of the street and back on the leash without having to fight it.

"And, um, we just got back from the vet because she, um, threw up a sock."

"A sock?"

"Yesssss."

There was a very pregnant pause.

"I don't understand how she would find a sock? I mean, you are keeping her in the kennel when she isn't directly training or playing with you. We talked about how important kennel training is. There is no way that she would be able to get ahold of a sock when she is constantly either supervised or kenneled."

I am suddenly ten years old and caught lying about cleaning my room. I panic and try to figure out how to throw the other members of my family under the bus.

"I don't know, either. I was just trying to take a shower and I left Zack and Petey in charge of her. . . . ." I trailed off.

Brad cleared his throat and saved me from the embarrassment of coming up with more excuses.

"You are going to have to watch her like a hawk. Once they start eating socks they won't stop until it is trained out of them. She gets a little bigger and she will be able to pass part of the sock through the stomach opening and you will have a nasty obstruction. Be careful." He left me with a stern warning and another set of training supplies to buy. The puppy snored in her kennel, exhausted from a day of excitement and cotton consumption.

Chapter 8

Puppy Postpartum, Low Blood Sugar, and Uncomforting Growls

A WEEK LATER I'M sitting in Dan's office trying to figure out why I've gained ten pounds, I'm irritable, and I also feel like I'm going to burst into tears at any moment. This is far above and beyond any normal PMS. That morning's breaking point was crying when I realized I forgot my coffee creamer coupled with being certain I had lost my keys. I also had a fresh crop of acne on my chin to offset the bags under my eyes. Dan patiently listened to me rant about how I was both losing my mind and also rapidly aging.

"Courtney," he finally said gently "Esther won't be little forever. There's a reason women your age don't typically have babies."

For crying out loud.

He's right.

I have postpartum depression about a puppy. She is waking me up at all hours of the night, has completely destroyed my morning routine, sucked up all of the time I usually spent exercising, and I worry about her constantly when I'm not with her. When my children were newborns I would obsessively sneak into their rooms at night because I was convinced I had put them into their cribs incorrectly somehow. With Esther I find myself driving home several times a day to make sure the kennel is correctly latched. This delights her, as she is ready to party whenever she lays eyes on me, which in turn puts me into the guilt spiral of leaving her home in her kennel, which turns into the same tears and shame that I felt when I was forced to leave my babies with a sitter. This dog is bringing out all of my mom crazy en force. I've had other puppies in my life and I've never been like this. I love Esther, but I don't necessarily love her more than I loved my other dogs. It's the pressure of having this very public dog who may or may not be the most important thing I do with my career. Bluntly put, if something happens to this dog I have to quit my job and leave the state. Probably change my name. I'm not sure if Zack will come with me. No pressure.

As February marched on Esther began spending more and more time on campus. The goal was to have her there three mornings a week to acclimate her to her new working environment. In hindsight, it was probably crazy for me to haul a three month old puppy to work with me at all. She could sit, sometimes, was mostly potty trained, and it was only four or five times a day I had to sprint down the hall to retrieve her after she decided she had had enough and made a break from my office. She continued to be a dumpster dog, sucking up everything on the ground with a frightening quickness. My upper back took on a gentle round as I marched her through campus trying to anticipate what trash she would try to hoover up next.

Yes, in hindsight it was crazy. But in the moment it felt like everything was just so sad and so hard and this was the best thing I could do to lighten the mood.

One day I had one of my sweetest students, Katie, turn up at my door. Katie is a Type One diabetic and was struggling with low blood sugar that morning. Her mom, a religion teacher at our school, had told her to just come and see Esther. I knew that low blood sugar feels really terrible and can make normally cheery and complacent kids become really unhappy and combative. Diabetes is one of those diseases that those unaffected tend to dismiss as "manageable," but the day to day life with it is really overwhelming. For years I had watched Katie and her family work to make sure that her diabetes did not impact her quality of life or prevent her from participating in things. I can't imagine the fear that comes along with all of the constant monitoring and the sleepless nights. I've always admired Katie and her mom for showing up at school full of positive energy and ready to change the world, when I knew from social media that they had suffered through a night of highs and lows together and were running on just a few hours of rest. While I was delighted to see Katie at my door, that quickly turned to sadness when I realized how just badly she felt. She was fresh from checking in with the school nurse and was now waiting for her sugar to stabilize before attempting class again.

"Come on in! Esther is in her kennel, but I am sure she'll be happy to see you."

Katie struggled to smile. I could see she was a little teary and was trying hard to maintain a pleasant attitude with me. She is unfailingly polite, even when she feels awful. She sat down on the couch in my office. Esther, who had up until this point on this day ignored visitors to my office to focus on her new nylabone, came chugging out of her kennel and straight into Katie's lap. Katie squealed as Esther wriggled around joyfully and then settled right down to snuggle. For the next fifteen minutes Katie quietly stroked Esther while the puppy sighed and lay very still, only moving to lift a leg in order to expose more belly to rub.

I was genuinely floored. It was the first time I had seen Esther react directly to a student in distress. She had charged around the room while crying students pet her whenever she came close enough or she had stared balefully up at me when captured in a hug. Never had she come out of her kennel in response to a sad student and laid herself down to receive their stress. It was amazing to watch and I found myself tearing up a little. The tears may have been the result of several months of broken sleep, but it was still a touching moment. I snapped a quick picture of Katie grinning widely while the little orange dog sat proudly in her lap.

Finished petting and obviously starting to feel better, Katie announced a while later that she wanted to check back in with our nurse one more time and maybe try going to class. She kissed Esther on the nose and bounded out of the room. As Esther settled back into her important work destroying the nylabone I texted the picture to Katie's mom.

Her response was quick and affirmed what I was hoping.

"WHAT," she replied. "Courtney, that is NOT what a low blood sugar episode looks like. I've never seen that kind of smiling while she's sick before."

It was encouraging. It was our first glimpse that maybe we were on to something. I posted the picture to Esther's Instagram and tried to get back to work.

With every encouraging moment, as setback usually followed. Breaking instinctive dog behaviors is arduous. For example, Esther isn't supposed to bark. She knows that. But sometimes they just build up in her. You can actually see it, like watching the spinning wheel of doom on a struggling Mac as something loads.

"Don't bark." I'll tell her firmly.

"I'm going to bark." Her face says it all.

"I mean it. We talked about this. Please don't bark." Sometimes I plead a little.

As we face each other in silence, her little black lip will start to curl up. "BARK!"

She's always embarrassed by it, appropriately. In an effort to contain her barks, she started growling at me to tell me what she wants. Her lip snarls and she low growls until she gets what she wants. It is basically the least comforting thing a dog can do. Although she has perfectly round dinosaur teeth that don't do much by way of intimidation, the grunts tend to spring me into action just to get the comfort dog to stop growling at me in public.

Esther always seemed to know when someone new was touring the school and would pick that time to begin her grunting and growling. She would wait until I was tethered to my office phone to begin her grumbling campaign, safely out of my reach because my phone cord does not stretch that far. It was as though she was born instinctively with the skill that all of us Gen X'ers developed from years of waiting until our parents were on the phone to meltdown just out of swatting range. Her grunts and growls were to alert me to the fact that she was ready to party outside, or collect cookies from the office ladies, or go check the tater tot bush again, or even just be done with day. I grew adept at stretching the phone out to snag her by a back leg and drag her into her kennel, with her protesting along the way.

Sometimes personal assistants to famous people come forward with shocking tell all stories. The public is always floored to find out that a beloved star is secretly abusive in private as the former assistant weaves a tale of being beaten with cell phones or privately cursed out.

I strongly identified with this. This was my life now. The adorable fuzzy comfort dog who was beloved by all was secretly terrorizing me.

Chapter 9

Every Dog Needs a Wolf Pack

BACK IN SUSA, QUEEN Esther is settling into her role as the wife of Xerxes. I have to imagine all of this came with a good deal of stress, after all this is the original rags to riches story. While skimming through her story, it truly does appear that she just shows up at the beauty pageant, captures the king's interest with her beauty, and it's all smooth sailing after that with just a little bit of insight from wise cousin Mordecai. Digging deeper, we see that the dear queen really had a tribe of cheerleaders.

When she arrived in the citadel for what was essentially the first round of the original Bachelor she was placed under the care of a eunuch named Hegai. Hegai was the first to take up Esther's cause, making sure that she received elaborate beauty treatments and special foods. He was a real life fairy godmother, transforming the girl into a glamorous woman and situating her in the best room with a staff to wait on her. He carefully coached her on what to say to the king and she took heart, eventually winning the favor of everyone who met her. Throughout the rest of the book the people surrounding Esther continue to look out for her and guide her. When Mordecai learns of Haman's plot to eradicate the Jews he takes to mourning, wearing a sackcloth and ashes and wailing bitterly. The officials around the palace took notice of his distress and instead of taking the safe route and staying uninvolved, they immediately set out to find Esther and get help.

The cousins had a wolf pack, if you will.

It's a cold and windy weekend in March. Esther, just over four months old, leaves for her first time at Brad Camp with Norton Dog Training in a few days and I am nervous about sending her off. Equally, I am excited for the chance to possibly sleep past 4:30 in the morning and to not live in fear of socks being left on the floor or holes being dug in the yard. While the mastiff is especially excited for the break from the puppy, it seems that no one needs it more than the cat. Desperate to be friends with Hobbes, Esther cannot seem to leave him alone. More desperate to not be friends with Esther, Hobbes has taken to spending his days hiding in my closet and doing unspeakable things to my shoes. I don't have the emotional space to worry about the cat's feelings right now, so I am hoping that it will all just settle down.

It's also the weekend of our first dance competition of the year. Both of my kids were dancing competitively at this point and the people at the dance studio had become our best friends over the years. On Friday night Zack and I dropped the kids off for a mandatory last minute practice and met a few of the other parents at the bar for happy hour.

Happy hour, um, got away from us. Relieved to be away from the sadness at work and the constant care of the dog, the night went on a little longer than it should have. Zack eventually navigated us back to get the kids and the other happy hour moms and I made our way into the dance hallway where we were greeted with chaos.

A small boy on the team barreled toward us wearing a pair of gray sweatpants that inexplicably had the word "AIDS" spray painted down the side.

"I'm AIDS," he crowed. "Evan is dyslexia and Petey is blind!" He sprinted away before I could process what he said.

The dance teacher appeared in the hallway holding what appeared to be a cheap sweatshirt and a can of black spray paint. The other, more obedient dance moms froze above the costumes they were working on and waited for her decree.

"Audrey isn't tall enough to be cystic fibrosis. I need a smaller disability." She turned and looked at me. I panicked and wished I had thought to grab a breath mint.

"M.S.?" It slipped out before I could stop it. She cocked her head to think for a second and then nodded.

"Go paint that on this." She shoved the sweatshirt and paint can at me and disappeared back into the dance room. I set about painting the shirt while trying to make frantic eye contact with the other renegade happy hour moms. One of the more obedient moms slipped in next to me, feverishly trying to dry the word "deaf" on a pair of tiny pants.

"I don't get it?" I screwed up my courage to try to figure out what was going on.

She shrugged. "There is a vision for this number. It's to the song from Greatest Showman about being true to yourself and overcoming obstacles. It's super moving. Originally the costumes were supposed to say things like "lonely" and "abandoned" but those didn't come in on time and so here we are."

I considered the kids huddled together in their artfully torn sweatsuits. "I'm not sure that I'm comfortable with "adopted," "aids," and "bullied" all lined up next to each other?"

"Then maybe you should've been here," she snapped under the pressure built from spending an entire evening scouring Wal-marts for matching sweatpants.

I snuck away to collect my newly blind and dyslexic children and flee. Down the hall, a conversation brewed about if this was actually politically correct. It was getting louder, but clearly not going to be resolved. I hustled the kids out to Zack like the coward that I am.

"Dyslexic?" He squinted in the dim parking lot.

"Don't ask." I threw the dance bags in the back and reminded him that we had a 6:30 am call time at the competition the next day.

Once home the children were marched through showers, what felt like several hundred bags of dance paraphernalia and snacks were packed, all socks were accounted for, Esther was safely ensconced once again in her kennel, and we all headed to bed to prepare for a ridiculously early wake up call. Zack was muttering to himself about having to spend an entire day sitting in the hallway of a theatre for what would amount to ten total minutes of the kids actually dancing. I was worrying about having lost costume pieces, if I could actually get fake eyelashes onto a ten year old, and how many faux pas my lack of filter had actually committed during the great costume debate. The puppy whined in her kennel, the cat raced back and forth across our bed, and a windstorm rattled the windows. An actual good night's sleep was not promising.

At 2am I woke up on the brink of a full-fledged panic attack, as I always do when I think I can have that second glass of wine. I tried to lay quietly next to Zack and slow my breathing down, but I was too sweaty and my heart was racing too quickly. I worried about everything from old student loans to missing jazz shoes to my parent's health, finally landing squarely on the fear that I had offended the dance teacher or the other moms or both. I stewed in my sweat puddle for almost an hour before deciding to abandon all hope and just head downstairs to watch TV. Unbeknownst to me, my dance mom friends were also all awake and worrying about the day.

Esther began grunting in her kennel to let me know that she was on to me being awake and was absolutely ready to party. Together with the cat we made our way to the living room, me in search of a good D list celebrity documentary, Esther in search of the cat, the cat in search of peace.

I settled onto the couch with a fuzzy blanket and a movie about Anna Nicole Smith. Esther circled the couch like a shark, hoping to get the cat to interact with her. Hobbes paced up and down the top of the couch, before landing squarely on my pelvis and pausing to look at me while I scratched his little tuxedo head.

"Hi, kitty!" I was delighted to see him.

He froze and an odd warmth spread through my blanket.

He peed on me. The cat peed through the blanket, onto me, and now the bitter stench of ammonia filled the air as the cat urine soaked into the feathers of the less than four year old Pottery Barn couch. I froze for longer than I would like to admit, before stripping down and shoving blanket and clothes in the washing machine. The puppy raced around in delight, while Hobbes took off for parts unknown.

Wrapped in an old towel, I began a frantic google search for how to get cat urine out of down feather filled furniture. The internet offered up a lengthy process involving baking soda, a water and vinegar mix, a vacuum, a several stage airing out process, and possibly the blood of a virgin. I threw on a pair of Zack's underwear and one of Evan's t-shirts, the only clean clothes in the laundry room, shoved Esther into the front living room where she promptly began chewing on the leg of the last remaining unscathed couch, and set to taking cushions apart. A little while later Zack appeared in the living room.

"What in the world. . .. . ." his voice trailed off as his took in the scene. Feathers gently floated in the air. The room smelled of cat pee and vinegar. Everything, including me, was covered in a vinegar and baking soda mash. I stood in his underwear and rubber gloves, holding a box of baking soda in one hand and a spray bottle in the other.

I shrugged. "I think the cat is mad about something? And we are going to need more baking soda."

By now it was nearing 3:30am. I had to have the kids up by five to get ready to go. I was still personally covered in cat urine and unsure if maybe this was just who I was going to have to be from now on.

Zack opened his mouth to speak, but was interrupted by the unmistakable sound of a puppy jumping on and off of furniture.

"You didn't kennel her?"

I didn't think it was a big deal, but as we both rounded the corner into the front living room I saw how grave of a mistake this actually was. This was actually a very big deal. Esther paused on the couch, ears cocked and tail wagging, delighted to see us.

Diarrhea spread from one side of the couch to other. The best we can figure is that she hopped up on the couch, pooped, then trampled up and down the length of the couch, spreading joy and loose stools. She hopped down and trotted over to us, leaving foul little footprints on the concrete floor.

I gingerly patted her head. "She's going to need another bath."

Zack appeared at a loss for words. The cat calmly strolled by to head upstairs while Zack's eyes swung from cat to dog to defiled couch to vinegar soaked cushions.

"I'm going for more baking soda." He slipped his shoes on and headed to the car. In the twenty years we have been together I have never been more concerned that he wasn't going to ever come home again. He drove off into the still dark morning while I dragged the puppy to the utility room sink for yet another bath. This was an exhilarating turn of events for Esther and she could barely contain her excitement as I lowered her into the water and tried not to think about what I was washing out of her fur.

While I was towel drying her, my phone began pinging with texts from the other dance moms, who had also been awake and worrying about the night before and the day ahead. Mutually, we were conflicted with the fear that we had caused hurt feelings but also the discomfort of putting our kids onstage in potentially offensive costumes.

"The sweatpants, though." Kimmy texted. "I've been up since two thinking about putting my kids on stage in front of people who potentially have these disabilities. And some of them aren't even disabilities?"

I hopped on the chat and gave them a brief summary of the horror I was currently surrounded with, beginning with Hobbes, describing the diarrhea, and admitting that we were a few hours into the nightmare and I still hadn't showered the cat urine off of myself. Minutes ticked by as the conversation dots appeared and disappeared. Clearly no one knew what social etiquette was for a time like this. Finally, Haley and Amber offered simple condolences and an offer to pick the kids up if we weren't going to all be competition ready in time. Kimmy, however, took a different route.

"Maybe we should get you your own disability sweatshirt? It could say 'my cat pees on me.'"

I wasn't ready to laugh about it yet. Not while the smells of dog poop and cat urine still battled for dominance in the rank air and feathers still floated around.

With cushions from the back couch drying, hopefully free from the scent of cat urine if the internet proved trustworthy, I started pulling the soiled cushion covers off of the front couch. Still wet from her bath, Esther paced the length of her puppy jail trying to catch my eye from behind the prison gates.

"Bad dog!" Drops flew as her butt wiggled with joy.

She managed to entirely miss the chaise area of the sectional couch while trampling her poop and I was relieved to not have to take that large cushion apart. I was working the covers into the washing machine when Zack showed back up, armed with even more snacks for the dance competition and a few dozen boxes of baking soda.

"How goes it?" He casually dropped the bags the on the counter and not so casually studied me for signs of nervous breakdown. I was still in his underwear, covered in baking soda, and probably smelling of cat pee. Hobbes reappeared on the stairwell and made his way to investigate the pulled apart sectional sofa.

"I don't know, I don't know. . . . ..wait. What is he doing?"

The cat had hopped up onto the sole remaining unmolested chaise cushion of the couch and paused, crouching low. Zack bolted toward him and he took off for the stairs. The unmistakable odor of fresh cat urine filled the air, mixing with the already foul stench permeating the house.

We both froze. I considered what our equity was in the house and if we could just move and start over fresh somewhere else, in a place where no one knew how disgusting we were. The cat screamed from my closet upstairs while the puppy spun in circles chasing a wet tail. Only the mastiff was peaceful, snoring in a corner, confident in the knowledge that she was the singular good animal in the house.

"Just go take a shower and get the kids up. Good luck with the competition. I'll stay here and try to get a handle on all of this."

Zack really is a hero.

I left him to his rubber gloves and the horrors of the couches and went up to try to rouse the kids, realizing along the way that I was so sleep deprived I could barely function. I tried to steady myself for a day of stage hair and makeup, costume pieces everywhere, hordes of children dancing to pop compilations, and my own children in offensive sweatpants. I bullied the children awake and then set about trying to scrub the cat urine smell off of my skin. The cat appeared to watch me shower like a tiny pervert, clearly reveling in the chaos he had caused.

With Zack and the animals all not speaking to each other, the kids and I filled my tiny Mini Cooper to the brim with an assortment of dance bags and snack coolers, all of which I would be required pack onto my body and haul through the venue like a reluctant Sherpa while the kids traipsed along like celebrities, greeting friends and polishing off breakfast sandwiches.

Along this journey, I ran into the mom who had been so irritated with me the night before.

"Look, I'm sorry. I totally appreciate you being dedicated and picking up the slack for losers like me who weren't there to help last night. I was taken aback by the costumes and I'm still not sure how I feel about the whole thing, but none of that has anything to do with you." I peered out at her from under all of the bags I was balancing as my daughter pranced by with an iced coffee she had procured from parts unknown.

"This is going to be a really beautiful message. It's good for our kids to think about people who are different from them." She was clearly still a little miffed.

"I don't disagree that they should, but I just question. . . . ." I let the thought hang in the air as our tiny male dancer sprinted by in his AIDS sweatpants. You could see parents from other studios turning to stare at his pants, as if they couldn't believe they had read it right.

We ended on a shaky truce. The day continued, marked by a series of escalating texts from Zack alternately declaring victory over the urine or sinking into despair that we were going to have to burn the house down and commit insurance fraud. I was sitting in the dark theatre with a pounding head googling "prison terms for arson" and "when good cats go bad" when my tribe of dance moms plopped down next to me.

"Our kids are up next. In their sweatpants. Try to watch the volume of your voice this time, the dance teachers are two rows over." They patted me and tried not to be too obvious about sniffing for any remaining urine odor.

We settled in for the number. It opened with our tiny boy in his AIDS pants. Soon the stage filled with children in tattered stenciled pants as in-spirational music filled the air. I began to shake with a case of the church giggles as the judges squinted at the stage in confusion. For the rest of the day, as they have so many times, my pack picked up my slack. They battled my daughter's hair while I researched carpet cleaning companies, fed my son while I fielded incoherent calls from Zack, and repeatedly assured me that we wouldn't be the smelly family forever.

Notably, for some reason no one was interested in sharing the snacks we brought from home that day.

In the end, our dance teacher had the last laugh. The number swept the competition, as it would every competition right up to winning best number at Nationals over the summer. It was a truly beautiful number with an inspiring message, although I wished the original costumes would have surfaced to replace the labeled sweat suits. Either way, I spent a lot of time of that dance season alternately trying to bite my tongue or suppressing church giggles.

When the day mercifully ended I went home to discover that Zack had triumphed. Order had been restored, the couches were reassembled, things smelled pleasant, and the puppy had air dried back into a round orange ball. Ironically, Esther's social media from that day shows an adorable puppy hugging her dad. No one would ever guess the amount of apology that should have come with that hug. Or that he is gripping her tight to keep her from trying to find the cat to make further amends.

Now to figure out what to do with the Hobbes. A trip to the vet confirmed that there was no medical issue. He didn't have a kidney or bladder infection, there was no quick medication fix. The vet helpfully suggested that he was unhappy about the arrival of the puppy, but did not have any suggestions as to how to keep him from destroying our house in his unhappiness.

I decided to consult my mom, who is a real life cat lady, feeding swarms of feral cats at an abandoned brick yard and occasionally catching wild cats to bring home and force to acclimate with the already alarming number of cats living in her house. No one knows for sure how many cats my mother actually has, in part because she is so shady about all of it. When I go back to Michigan to visit there is a rotation of cats, with usually four roaming the house and an undetermined number of others at "camp." Her basement contains enough cages to get her on a government watch list and it isn't unusual to hear her bragging about "almost being able to pet a new cat without the glove."

I'm not sure what the glove is. I haven't asked. I picture it like a falconer's glove that she uses to stroke wild hissing cats. I'm also not sure where the cat mania came from. We never had a cat growing up. No one ever liked cats. The only reason Zack and I have a cat is because I had a meltdown during a scorpion infestation one summer and read that cats would alert you to the presence of scorpions.

If you're wondering, this is a lie.

I digress.

I called my mother, the cat lady, to see what she thought we should do with Hobbes. My mother sees herself as a champion rescuer of homeless cats. She had lots of suggestions, most of which left Zack shaking his head and continuing to google the policies of local cat rescues.

"More litter boxes. He just needs more litter boxes. Bigger ones. You should probably give him the entire laundry room. And I bet he'd like cat trees upstairs and downstairs. Some new toys. Have we talked about shelves? And really you should be taking some time off of work to focus on him. He's just unhappy. You need to figure out how to make him happy and he'll quit peeing on stuff."

Zack rejected the idea of a house full of cat trees, but we did compromise and place a new large litter box in the laundry room. The cat refused to go near it. My sleep became even more interrupted as now in addition to being woken up several times a night to take Esther out, I jolted awake every time the cat jumped up on the bed and then lay there frozen and hoping to not get peed on. In time, Hobbes began using his new box, forged a friendship with Esther, and earned back my trust by not peeing on me. Even better, Esther left for her first round of Brad camp, leaving Hobbes and Maeby to return to their peaceful coexistence.

This tale may have included far more foul fluids than necessary to illustrate the importance of a good circle of friends. If you don't have a group of friends that you can text at 2am to admit that you are covered in cat urine and your entire house may be a hazmat risk, it is time to get more vulnerable and work on deepening your connections. As life continued to throw relentless tragedies at our school community and I struggled to determine how to support everyone around me, those three women basically strapped me onto their backs and dragged me through life. They made sure my children never wanted for anything, listened to me for hours on end, and ran countless miles with me as I tried to process through everything.

When we see someone struggling we are quick to ask what we can do. I can tell you that the most emotionally intelligent thing to do is just show up. I am forever grateful to Kimmy for showing up and putting me in her car and walking me through buying a funeral dress when I was too paralyzed to do it myself. I am grateful to Amber for showing up to scoop my kids up and endlessly distracting them when I was too overwhelmed. I'm grateful to Haley for showing up to put in hours of both venting and tough love, never letting me wallow when I got down. Showing up looks like all sorts of different acts, but it's entirely about being present and reliable.

When Esther's tribe came to let her know of Mordecai's distress she immediately showed up for him, although it may not have initially looked like showing up. She first sent him new clothes to replace the sackcloth. When he refused those, she dispatched a eunuch to find Mordecai and report back to her what had her cousin so upset. He carefully detailed what had happened and included the upsetting edict that Xerxes had allowed.

This had to be terrifying news to receive. So terrifying that Esther, who had been hiding her Jewishness all along, immediately responded from a place of defensiveness and self-preservation. Her response to Mordecai points out that no one can appear before the king without invitation and that she herself had not been summoned to see him in almost a month. I am sure her head was spinning with all of the reasons why she wasn't the right person for the job. And this response caused Mordecai to reply in Esther 4:14 with the verse that has captured my heart:

"For if you remain silent at this time, relief and deliverance for the Jews will arise from another place, but you and your father's family will perish. And who knows but that you have come to your royal position for such a time as this?"

I love this butt kicking, but I also love Esther's response. She replies with her own request; for Mordecai to gather up all of the Jews in Susa to spend three days fasting and praying for her as she prepared to face her fears and approach the king. We need our people to pray for us and believe in us and show up for us in order for us to face our hard things.

Chapter 10

Trying to Just Show Up

NEVER ONE TO GO quite peacefully, the morning before Brad camp Esther discovered a planter in the backyard with a broken sprinkler head. Which meant mud. It turns out that mud is about the most delightful thing that can happen to a puppy. By the time we discovered what was happening, mud was caked into her hair and she was grinning from ear to ear. I dragged her into the house and threw her into the shower where she sat staring mournfully out at me. Dirt swirled around the shower drain. I blew her dry into a giant fluff and counted the hours until Brad would come to collect her.

Esther had a ball her first round of Brad camp. He was also raising her cousin, Brimstone, and the two of them had a series of adventures together that Brad was careful to periodically update me on. It was a lot like sending a child to camp and waiting for the camp to post pictures on social media. I received pictures of Esther swimming in the lake, Esther and Brim running through the desert, Esther sitting proudly on an agility stool, Esther walking peacefully on a leash. I was struck by the fact that not only did she seem like a new dog, but that she seemed to be having more fun than I have on my vacations. Brad deposited her back to me two weeks later with a stern warning not to undo all of his hard work.

"She sits, she stays, she places where you tell her. She runs right into her kennel when you tell her to kennel. She is confident on the leash. Please stay consistent with her. Please don't ruin her progress."

He rumbled off in his giant truck with Brimstone riding shotgun. Esther and I looked at each other. She had the same look in her eyes that my kids have when they return from a sleepover with a family that is more fun than ours. Hope that I was about to create an adventure for her, resignation that I probably was not. She was right. There would be no lake or mountain adventures any time soon, just lots of leashes and kennels and crying kids hoping for a chance to pet her at school.

I did try hard not to undo all of Brad's hard work after this and all subsequent training sessions. I know as I type this that if he ever reads these words he will probably put his head in his hands and sigh heavily. While he's never come right out and said it, I am pretty sure Brad equally adores and wants to punch me. And possibly Esther. I've referred friends to Brad to have their own dogs trained and they all report that Brad talks about Esther the same way that people talk about annoying little sisters.

"She's just . . . a lot of dog." I'm told he will say resignedly when asked about her.

But oh, did we try. While I want to love structure and routine, I am not necessarily the most disciplined and that certainly spilt over onto Esther. If we had been in a typical school year and I would have had the emotional space and the time to leave Esther at home during the day and work hard together at night I think we would have had a better chance. Instead I hauled her into work with me at such a young age, often too distracted by my job to consistently correct the behaviors that drove Brad crazy. In those moments I felt a crushing guilt and a sense of total failure. Here was one more thing in my life that I felt was smoke and mirrors, that I was trying and failing.

In hindsight it worked out, as these things tend to do. I know Brad winces a little when he sees Esther and I can't blame him. But all things considered, Esther growing up at Faith has resulted in a quirky little dog who sees the campus as her home and a place to have both work and fun. She knows the daily routine, slouching off to morning devotions with me off of her leash and stopping to greet excited 6th graders on the way. She knows when we take off the vest that it's time to play fetch and get excited. She also knows which office ladies hide dog treats in their drawers and that it is possible to sneak off for treats if I am distracted on the phone. I continue to try to correct those behaviors with both Esther and the grown-ups. She is a shameless cookie hound.

I don't know that I would consistently take Esther to work in other places, beyond simple visits. She is not, as Brad reminds me, "tightened up enough" in her behaviors. She still gives me the occasional tug on the leash, still can get a little excited when she sees another dog, and still has a deep seated belief that she is entitled to any loose tater tots she comes across.

These are all factors that I can control at Faith, minus the occasional tater tot. She did find a tot in a bush one day, which she insists on revisiting often because hope springs eternal that this is a magical tater tot bush. I can live with these quirks, especially because I see her daily set her dog desires aside to do the work I ask of her.

And who doesn't love a tater tot every now and then?

With Esther showing signs of being trained, March turned into April and we collectively held our breath that the end of this horrible school year was drawing closer. Things had been calming a little in the counseling offices. Our girls were more consistently making it through the day and the issues that we were dealing with had a little more normalcy; parent/teacher miscommunications, drama surrounding the breakups of torrid middle school love affairs, or spring fever struck high school students attempting to skip classes. I think we were all grateful for the chance to be annoyed by the annoying again. I was finding myself struggling to deal with this normalcy. After so many truly traumatic issues and seeing kids in so much genuine pain, it was becoming difficult to downshift and give the kind of weighty attention to issues that felt minimal to me but important to others. I know that I frustrated more than one parent by being unable to support or understand their emotional escalation regarding whichever minor issue their child was facing. My counseling style has always been to allow people to express whatever they needed, acknowledge the frustration behind it, and try to gently guide them to another perspective. I found myself unable to drum up the patience for this process. I've carried this lesson with me whenever I am faced with someone who appears to be wholly unhelpful. We just never know what emotions the person before us is trying to process.

In some ways I greatly regret this time because I did not build potential relationships. In other ways, it was an important lesson to me as a counselor, that I do not have to emotionally affirm everyone on everything all of the time. I was also walking through the guilt that so many third responders struggle with, that the emotion I am diffusing every day from the PTSD afflicted is not my own and their trauma is not my trauma, yet I am emotionally exhausted. Acknowledging that exhaustion brings with it a special kind of guilt that is further draining. The cycle goes on and on and is difficult to break without intervention.

Just as we felt things were calming down, we were struck with another tragedy. A freshman was killed in a very freak car accident while driving home from dinner with a cousin. A tire flew off of another car on the highway and came crashing into theirs, killing them both instantly. Only the cousin's boyfriend survived. This student, while not popular in the traditional sense, was quirky and effusive and a well-known figure on this campus. I have many memories of him as middle schooler, wearing giant glasses and a huge scarf and not understanding why I didn't want him to draw cartoons all over his standardized test scantrons or why I needed him to stop egging on his grumpy English teacher. Our school was rocked. It felt as though the last remaining unaffected portion of our campus had finally been afflicted. The population impacted by 1 October was largely upperclassmen. Our faculty grieved the loss of our teacher's son. And now our younger kids were faced with a loss of their own.

We received the news of his death early on a Sunday morning. The coroner made first contact with my principal and a little while later a parent close to the family called me. I sat at our tiny kitchen table with Zack, trying to figure out what happens next. The puppy stole toys from the mastiff and raced around the house trying to entice her to play. Maeby and I both sighed heavily.

"I'm going to get cleaned up and head over to their house and see what I can do."

Zack nodded and Evan suggested that I bring Esther with me. At the sound of her name, she popped her head up, revealing the toy batting stuck to her beard from destroying yet another supposedly indestructible toy.

"Probably not a good idea. . ."

I drove to the family's house, honestly terrified. While I preach showing up, I am ironically not good at just showing up for those that I don't know well. There are those beautiful people who don't bat an eye at coming to someone's home to offer comfort. They tend to bring food, know what to say, and are confident enough to start rooting around an unfamiliar kitchen to look for extra serving spoons. Trained counselor or not, I am not that kind of confident. My social anxiety tells me that I am intruding and I have no business involving myself. I stumble over my words, don't know what to do with my arms, and convince myself that everyone in the room is wondering just who I think I am to show up where I'm not wanted. I am genuinely jealous of the women who are able to insert themselves into any home, any situation, any family and be helpful. Showing up in uncertain relationships had been a long struggle for me, and little did I know how the year of 2018 was going to break me of that.

The scene I walked into when I arrived was one of sheer heartbreak. Friends surrounded the couple as they grieved the loss of their only child. I hugged his mother while she wept. I knew that this boy had been her whole life. She had abandoned a highly respected career and put her twelve years of college aside as she planned his favorite meals, picked him up each day from school, hounded him about school work, and was a presence on our campus. This is a woman who truly delighted in motherhood and it was evident to all of us who knew her. Frantic for something to say, I started telling my stories of him; all of the times he made me laugh or want to pull my hair out. Tentative laughter rang out as others told their stories. I started to take note of which parents were there to offer support, so I could get a handle on which children would be most affected. I arrived home a few hours later to find an obedient puppy sitting prettily by the door.

"I spent the day working with her. I know you need her to have it together tomorrow, so I tried to get her head on straight." Zack is the best. I don't know how to ask for what I need, yet somehow he always knows. On this day what I needed was someone to spend time on dog training and a hug. I wrapped myself in his arms while the puppy circled our ankles, oblivious to what the morning would bring.

The next day Esther and I headed into school, she blissfully unaware of what the day would hold and me praying under my breath and wiping sweaty hands on my pants. The day unfolded much as I anticipated. Sobbing children rocketed through my door and held Esther tightly while I comforted them and asked for their memories of their friend. Some were angry, some were questioning God, some were anxiety stricken, all of them were just heartbroken. This kid was such a part of campus life and my students struggled to figure out what their new routines would look like without him. Esther hung in there, taking the hugs and periodically rolling onto her back to invite belly-rubs. Kids smiled through tears as she exposed her little fried chicken belly and stared up at them hopefully.

That week passed in another blur of tears. The school took over planning the funeral to spare the grief stricken family. On the day of the service I sat in the car with Esther trying to pep talk her.

"We've talked about this. You absolutely cannot bark. I don't know how else to say it. You need to sit like a good girl, let people pet you, and lay quietly. Can you do it?"

Just now six months old, she peeped up at me from under her overgrown bangs. She did not appear confident.

"I mean it. You have to sit. I brought your blankie and a toy but you have to get it together. Do you have it together?"

Esther avoided eye contact by shifting in her seat to look out of the window. She seemed to be considering the request.

"Let's go."

Heart racing and anxiety pumping, I hauled the fluffy puppy into the lobby of our chapel. She was greeted by a crowd of teary children and responded by immediately flopping onto her back and stretching out for belly rubs. The kids patted her as they filed into the service, a few stopping to kneel and hug her. She stared up at me, a little smug, as if to make sure I noticed what a good job she was doing. I snuck her a treat and dragged her into the sound-booth with me. I was going to run the visuals for the service and the sound-booth had the added bonus of potentially helping to disguise any canine tantrums. I cried silent tears throughout the funeral, while Esther lay on her blanket chewing contentedly on her bone. Every so often she paused to stare up, as if she wasn't sure what her role as comfort dog was when it came to me.

Chapter 11

The Comfort Dog Gave Me Pink Eye

THROUGHOUT SPRING OF 2018 Esther worked half days in my office. She would come in three or four days a week, either in the morning or in the afternoon, and practice being a school dog. Fortunately, she was becoming a pretty casual part of campus life. While still adorable, she no longer looked like a live teddy bear scurrying around and had gained enough weight and grown large enough to be substantial enough to really snuggle with. The kids adored her. So did most of the adults and the traffic in my office increased dramatically with people hoping to spend some time with her. I welcomed the attention for her, but found myself struggling with having my work interrupted several times an hour to make small talk with coworkers who thought it rude to not talk to me while petting the dog. Eventually we all came to an understanding that it's fine to pet Esther and ignore me. Esther thrives on the attention and I really do not.

This was one of the obstacles that no one prepared me for. I knew that I would potentially have to deal with kids creating issues for an excuse to come to my office and pet the dog. I tried to ward this off by making sure that Esther was present in as many places on campus as possible. There is no need to duck out of English just to come pet the dog if you were able to give her a hug in the hallway on the way to class. Adults took a little more finesse. I desperately wanted everyone to love the dog and have ownership. I desperately did not want everyone to feel like they had to find things to chat with me about in order to pet her. I finally had to just be transparent; it's ok, pet the dog, I'm going to work on these emails. I started handing her leash off to people I knew were very vested in her and she became used to cruising campus with handlers other than me.

One day in early May as we loaded Esther into the car for school I notice that her left eye looked a little red. I figure she probably took a stick to the eye while pulling one of our bushes out of the ground that morning, as was still her routine to the chagrin of Zack, and didn't think too much of it. We headed into my office where she was finally going to work a full day. She laid in my doorway peering hopefully out just waiting for people to come and pet her. She had taken to laying on her belly at the entrance to my office like an alligator, creeping toward the hall and hoping to be noticed.

Our curriculum director walked by that afternoon and did a double take.

"What's wrong with her eye?"

I lifted her frizzy orange bangs and found a gunky, red, swollen eye. We had managed to go two solid weeks without a trip to the vet, so it made total sense that we would be due.

I texted my son to meet me in my office when he finished a hard day of seventh grade so he could help me drag her to the vet.

"What's wrong?" he responded.

"I think she has pink eye. Dog pink eye. I googled it."

"That's a thing?" I could hear his skepticism over his text.

"Yes, so don't let her touch your eyes with her paws. The last thing I need is for the comfort dog to give you pink eye."

"I'll make a note of that."

He turned up in my office an hour later and we loaded our sticky round ball of a dog into the car, careful to keep her away from our eyes. She returned to the vet a conquering hero, delighted to be back among the adoration of the vet techs.

"Giardia? Or more socks?" we were greeted. "Is it the cat again?"

"No. . . I think she has pink eye."

After several hours she was diagnosed with conjunctivitis and we were sent home with another bill and an assortment of drops and creams. Esther came home delighted to share her adventures with her big mastiff sister, while we struggled to keep her away from the other dog's eyes.

Prone to pink eye or not, Esther was starting to catch on. The local news routinely featured stories on her, reaching out to see what we were up to when things were slow or they needed a feel-good piece. I was beginning to travel more to talk about what starting a dog program was like, even though it was still such a work in progress. This kind of attention was great, and I was encouraged that other schools would follow suit, but what I really loved was hearing how she touched individual kids.

Any school official can tell you that it happens routinely; I will wander in from the melee of supervising kids after school or trying to convince drivers to follow the pick-up line rules to find a parent waiting in the office for me. I usually have to take a deep breath and try to get centered before greeting the parent, because rarely do these meetings bring good news. Parents do not typically battle after school traffic, score a parking spot, and head into the front office to tell me that I'm doing a good job. When those compliments come they arrive in emails sent from iPhones while waiting in the car line. Parking and coming inside means that there has been a sudden drop in grades, a conflict between friends, or a child being cut from an athletic team or play.

It's not usually my favorite way to end a day.

The mom waiting for me on this particular day was a striking blonde, tall and cheery. Esther and I greeted her in the lobby and she did the appropriate amount of fawning over the dog. Freshly naked, being freed of her working vest at the end of the day, and tired from a rousing game of fetch with the 6th graders Esther tolerated being petted by the woman while looking at me from the corner of her eye. She always behaves as though I've deeply betrayed her when she has to sit still to greet people after her vest comes off. This dog has drawn a firm line between on and off duty, the vest being her punch-clock. And once she is clocked out she is resentful at any bit of anything she perceives as work. I tried to give her stern enough stink eye to keep her in line without appearing crazy to the mom. I don't think it worked.

"Esther is actually why I'm here. I just needed to tell you. . .. . ." The woman trailed off when Esther buried her face against her leg and snuggled in. "She's just so sweet."

Sweet. Esther is sweet but she also plays the room like a fiddle. I don't know how she knows when to turn it on, but she will routinely collapse in a no bones fashion against visitors, inciting gasps and giggles, all while giving me a wicked side eye. Her orange belly fully exposed, she will lay on peoples' feet and shamelessly shill for belly rubs. As a working dog, she fully understands it's against her "working rules" but she also somehow realizes that I can't pull her off of a visiting parent or a giggling child without looking like a psycho.

"So sweet!" The mom collected herself and kept one hand on Esther. "I have a 6th grade boy who is notorious for not talking to us. Ever since he started school it has been pulling teeth to get him to tell us anything at all about his day. He would get in the car after a day at elementary school and I was lucky to get one word answers about anything."

I nodded, having my own introverted boy at home. I'm actually at school with him and I still have no idea what he does for most of the day. Sometimes our only common ground is what the cafeteria served for lunch.

"Esther has changed all that," she continued. "He gets in the car and all I have to ask is if he saw Esther that day. He tells me about where he saw her, who he was with, what they were doing. He tells me if he pets her or not. If he saw her at chapel then he tells me about what happened in the chapel service. If it's a day that he didn't run into her, then we look up her Instagram and he tells me about what she was doing in her story. I've never gotten so many details out of him."

She paused and Esther gently nudged her to continue petting. "I know that you guys all know how great she is here and how much the kids love her. But I don't know if you realize her. . . . ..sphere of influence. How much she actually helps families."

Sphere of influence? Exciting to hear, but bold words when they concern a forty pound drama queen who only yesterday was rampaging on my couch because she hated her new sweater.

The woman shared that they were getting their son a Goldendoodle puppy for Christmas. They've never had a dog before, never thought about having a dog before, but were excited for the family bonding this pup would bring. I congratulated her on the new addition and asked that she send me a picture of boy and puppy's first meeting. She gave Esther a final pat and headed out. After she left Esther hopped up on my office couch, tongue hanging comically to one side, and began kicking the pillows to the ground to let me know she was ready to go home.

Sphere of influence indeed.

Chapter 12

Charlee

THIS IS PROBABLY THE hardest part of the story of the 2017–2018 year, certainly the most shocking and greatly traumatic. There was a lot of waffling on my part as to how or if to include it, because it hurts to talk about and it isn't even my story to tell. I wrote and deleted, deleted and wrote, with this chapter not included in the original draft I sent out for editing. A few days ago over lunch with Dave, the one whose story it is to tell, he encouraged me to include Charlee; that her life needs to be shared, talked about, and celebrated. As with most hard things, our human nature is to avoid talking about them in order to keep from making things feel awkward or because we just don't know what to say and we are afraid we will offend. As Dave has repeatedly and wisely told me, not saying the name or telling the story of loved ones who have passed on is far more hurtful to those left behind than accidentally saying the wrong thing.

Dave is Dave of the perennially popular social studies teacher fame. He's the guy that connects with all of the kids, especially the hard to reach ones, and the one that alumni tend to seek out over social media when they find themselves in need of a mentor. He's the popular affable guy, the one who played college baseball and went on to become our Varsity coach. For all of his successes and his way with people Dave should be, on paper anyway, kind of arrogant and standoffish. He just isn't. He is sweet and compassionate and remarkably emotionally intelligent.

Dave is also a devoted family man, relishing the role of husband to Niki, his beautiful wife, and father to his growing family. It was common to see him out on the baseball field directing players while his tow headed toddler, Cooper, trailed behind with a baseball in hand. Baby Charlee, a true firecracker born on the 4th of July, had joined Cooper in 2017. As dark haired as Cooper was light, this little girl captured the hearts of all of Dave's coworkers, students, and players. The adorable pair made appearances at all of our school functions, with Cooper taking his role as big brother very seriously as he watched over his pretty little sister.

It is odd in Vegas to have rainy and chilly days as April turns into May. This particular day, not long after we had held the service to remember our student who passed in the car accident, a dismal day greeted the valley. It was sprinkling and cold enough that I remember wearing a Faith windbreaker over my button down blouse for the day. The weather didn't stop a baseball game from happening, so Dave had dropped Charlee off at their babysitter's house while Niki worked her nursing shift. A gentle woman who was married to one of our theology teachers ran an in home daycare for some of the staff kids.

I was packing up my office for the day that May 2nd, a day that Esther had stayed home, when the call came in to my middle school principal, Sarah, that something had happened to Charlee. The babysitter had called the school and been patched through to Human Resources to notify Dave. After calling him at his baseball game our HR lady called Sarah to let her know that first responders were on the way to the sitter's house. Sarah, Scott, and I briefly gathered in the hallway and together decided to head over ourselves and see what, if anything, we could to do help.

Sarah cried quietly. "I think she's passed away. I think the baby died." Scott drove in a grim silence. Dave, who did not have his vehicle at the baseball field, had taken his assistant coach's truck. This meant that we beat him to the house by a few minutes and were standing in the driveway as he pulled up. Niki arrived soon after, having a longer drive from the hospital.

The hours that followed are hard to describe. Emergency medics and detectives took command of the scene. Charlee had been laid down to nap in a bassinet and had quietly quit breathing. Although the babysitter did her best with CPR and called for help right away, it was just too late. Helplessly, I watched as Dave came outside with Cooper, sitting the little blonde boy in his lap and hugging him close as he whispered to him. Repeating the promises of the Bible that we hold dear and take comfort in, I did my best to console the babysitter with her husband, praying that the peace of God would be felt. The air was thick with guilt and grief and pain. Eventually, there was nothing more to be said in the moment. I hugged Dave tightly and told him how much I loved him, which I still do although now I admire him just as much as I love him.

As we know, even in the times that God appears to be absent He is forever present. There are no coincidences in our lives and in even the most unspeakable moments of pain God provides sources of human comfort. Dave's closest cousin is a firefighter/paramedic here in Las Vegas. On this particular cold and drizzly day he had been guilted into taking an overtime shift to cover for someone out sick at a station he never had been assigned to before. He was the first responder to this scene, the one to work on Charlee and his familiar voice the first that Dave heard upon arriving. As the hours wore on, he occupied Cooper by allowing him to play in the firetruck to distract him. Life on this side of heaven hurts, thankfully God plants people in the right place at the right time to try to ease that pain.

Just a week later Scott and I drove together to the most heartbreaking funeral I have ever attended. A slideshow ran pictures of adorable Charlee as Johnny Cash's "A Boy Named Sue" played, a song Dave frequently sang to his beautiful little girl with her traditionally male name. The faculty at Faith had spent the week leading up to the funeral in the same way that we would spend the ensuing weeks; just showing up as best we could. Dave and Niki's house was filled with people and food, all trying in every way to show as much love and support as possible. Following the funeral Scott and I drove out with a small group of gatherers to the graveside service. Dave's family is old Las Vegas, descended from the original settlers of St. Thomas, a city that was relocated when it was submerged underwater to make room for Lake Mead. The family burial site is breathtaking, on a beautiful cliff overlooking acres and acres of land. Wind gently rustled the trees around us as Charlee was laid to rest in an area fitting for a feisty little princess.

Understandably, Dave stayed home for the last month of the school year. He and I were in touch consistently with texts and when Dan and I would show up awkwardly at Dave and Niki's home. We would bring tales of the school day, comical snippets of whatever trivial school drama was unfolding, and watch Cooper careen around the house waving his beloved Golden Knights towel. During those weeks Dave stayed focused on his wife and boy while we tried at school to help the students deal with the grief they felt on behalf of one of their favorite teachers. Death is hard for kids to process. This kind of loss, especially at the end of year marked by so much trauma, felt impossible to work through. The students were sad and angry on Dave's behalf and did not know what to do with all of that emotion. I honestly didn't know what to do with all of it, either.

Dave did return to school in the fall and while the kids and adults alike were relieved and happy to have him back, it was hard. Reminders of that day and other triggers were lurking everywhere. Much like our girls from the concert, it was difficult for him to anticipate when a day would become overwhelming, when grief would strike, and when paralyzing anxiety would set in. Dan and I did our best to support, to sit silently and listen, to use humor to diffuse when it felt appropriate, to just show up.

I don't know how one heals from losing a child. Putting one foot in front of the other and continuing on in the wake of such a loss sounds Herculean. I genuinely pray that Dave writes that book about healing one day. He has the quiet wisdom and faith to help a lot people. Sitting at lunch together mulling over the last few years, he encouraged me to include Charlee not only so that her story could be told but so that anyone who reads this could hear the hopeful message that healing does occur and good times can follow the most devasting of heartbreak. As we talked Petey herded Cooper and his new little brother, just a year old, around the patio of the restaurant. Happy laughter and shrieking rang out as they discovered the fountain in the corner.

"Besides, it's a book about Esther and Esther was a big part of helping when I came back to work." Dave smoothly passed off a french fry to his youngest as he sailed by with Petey on his heels.

I snorted. "She was a mess."

Dave disagreed. He remembers Esther being able to pick up on the mood when he came into my office. If he was feeling ok or struggling just a little to maintain control of his emotions and seeking some distraction she was her typical goofy self, clambering over him on the couch or showing him a toy she had snuck into her kennel. He remembers her coming to lay quietly and lean on him in the times that he was overwhelmed and breaking down. I guess I remember that, too. She bonded so differently to the people that I am close with at work, people that she saw routinely but who didn't usually need much from her. Prior to the loss of Charlee Dave was an exciting potential playmate for her, a guy that typically had an extra baseball somewhere on him and who was always down to pet her a little bit more enthusiastically than what was dignified. As he struggled with returning to work she learned to pick up his mood and respond accordingly, reading the room better than most adults.

After the worry about if training a dog to just keep on campus was selfish or not an effective use of a Comfort Dog, it was good to see her being so comfortable with her people that she could adapt her responses to them. Dave Enters was right; it is helpful to have a canine responder who is already familiar to everyone before tragedy strikes.

As we packed up the kids to head from lunch, discreetly kicking loose french fries under the fountain's base, Dave and I chatted a little more about

Charlee as we headed to the parking lot. While the hope of healing after loss is such a valuable gift, that isn't the note that this chapter needs to end on. It needs to end on this:

Charlee is important. She lived a big a life in ten months.

Charlee matters, Charlee is loved, and Charlee will always be remembered.

Chapter 13

Esther's First Summer and When to Cry Uncle

WHEN THE 2017/18 SCHOOL year mercifully ended the last week of May, Brad scooped Esther back up and took her home with him for some intensive training as I made the rounds of 8th grade promotion, baccalaureate, graduation, dance recitals, and graduation parties. Having him collect her was a gift, as it saved me from making excuses as to why she wasn't attending any of these events or, even worse, trying to sit through a two hour baccalaureate service with a seven month old puppy.

People always asked me if it was hard to be separated from Esther for more than a week at a time while she went to camp, but I think we were honestly ready for the break from each other when it rolled around. Even better was her sheer delight at the sound of Brad's voice. I loved how happy she still was to go with him. She would leap about in delight while I would attempt to earn his approval by trying to force her to do something to prove I hadn't totally undone his work while breathlessly ranting a stream of stories about her interactions with kids.

While she was delighted to go with him, it is entirely possible that he was a little relieved every time he got in his truck and left our house. The times that she was extra naughty at pick up I would follow him out to the truck trying to force him to look at Instagram pictures proving that she mostly behaved at work. It is a testament to Brad's character that he still speaks to me at all. This time there were other dogs at Brad Camp with her, in addition to Brad's own impeccably trained personal dogs. I would get pictures every day of Esther swimming or hiking with her new wolf pack. Her big dopey grin would beam out from the center of the pack, clearly delighted with both her new friends and her adventures. You could see her gaining confidence in herself in each picture. While she enjoyed the mastiff and pined after the cat's affections, she obviously relished this new community of dog friends all led by her hero, Brad.

A week later she was back, along with another stern lecture about not undoing Brad's hard work with her. I crossed my heart and promised that now that I was off for the summer I would redouble my efforts and focus all of my attention on training. Brad rolled his eyes and rumbled off with a new doodle riding shotgun. Around the same time, I received a message on Esther's Instagram inviting her to be a part of an event run by a local non-profit organization.

Gracie's House, here in Las Vegas, is a delightful organization that hosts inclusive activities for people of all different ability levels. Founded by the mother of a sweet girl with Down's Syndrome, they organize everything from cooking classes to CrossFit events. Everyone is welcome and the environment is always warm and inviting. This June they were planning an event where everyone would get to ride the High Roller, the giant and terrifying wheel that stands out on the Vegas strip, followed by a dinner event afterwards. The founder noted that some of the kids were afraid of riding the wheel and wondered if Esther might come along to offer some comfort. I read her text message and considered Esther, who was again racing around the house taunting the mastiff with a stolen toy. Take a seven month old puppy to the strip to meet with a group of people I didn't know? And ride a tourist attraction? Also, dinner in a restaurant?

I knew better than to run this by Brad. Or my husband. I hastily committed to the event before I could think of all of the reasons I shouldn't and ordered her a new service dog vest so she would look extra fancy. A week later I loaded kids and dog into my Mini Cooper and set about trying to navigate my way to the strip. I am afraid to drive to downtown on a good day. In a car with kids and dog on the way to a public event with a puppy that I did not completely trust was a whole new level of fear and sweaty feet. After several wrong turns we finally found the correct parking garage and I sat taking deep breaths while the others jostled for space in the tiny car. I would occasionally see Esther's orange head sail by in the rearview mirror as she fought the kids.

"Ok. Let's do it. Let's see how it goes."

The only way to describe the way the four of us entered the High Roller is rumbled. I kept Esther tightly on her leash while she tried to take in everything around her. People would yell "DOG" and point at her as we passed and my kids began to circle around her like preteen bodyguards. She was clearly confused about what we were doing and I was starting to feel like she might be right to be worried. My fears were confirmed when she suddenly squatted and pooped outside of the entrance. I tried to gracefully and discreetly clean up the mess while drunken tourists stumbled by taunting me. Sloppy men hooted and hollered while the puppy circled my legs with her leash. I tied off the stinking bag and briefly considered throwing it at them. My daughter, never one to back down from a fight, wound up shaking her fists and yelling back at them like a tiny old man defending her lawn. We eventually found the event and Esther redeemed herself by laying complacently on the floor and accepting pets from dozens of kids and adults. She seemed delighted to find herself doing familiar work in an unfamiliar and unexpected place. With the last child appropriately comforted and loaded into a Ferris wheel pod, I started getting Esther ready to leave.

"What are you doing? Come on up and ride the High Roller with all of us!" The founder of the organization was gesturing wildly at us. My kids stared up at me hopefully.

"Are you sure? I'm not sure her manners will last for an entire hour trapped in a pod?"

"It'll be fine! What's the worst that could happen?"

Trying not to remember the great poop trampling of earlier in the year, I smiled weakly and the four of us headed in. Esther was a gem for the entire hour. A little girl riding in our pod was diagnosed nonverbal autistic. She crouched next to Esther gently squeezing orange tufts of hair and occasionally patting her nose while Esther stared up at her adoringly. The two of them were so cute that I forgot to take in the stunning views of the strip at sunset.

The feeling in the pod and in the restaurant afterward is still hard to describe. Camaraderie for sure, but at a whole new level. It was the kind of strength in numbers that comes with collective experience. The riders and their families had weathered all of the obstacles and triumphs that come with being differently abled and clearly found joy in the camaraderie of the group. More than that though, was the sense that everyone could just let down defenses and enjoy time. I don't know if you've ever found yourself in a group where it is next to impossible to make a social error and everything about you is embraced. If you haven't, I suggest you try it. It was a magical evening of sincere love and support.

When the night was over, after we bid our farewells, the kids and I chattered excitedly about Esther's work all the way to the car. I was so excited that I only cried from the traffic once while trying to navigate my way home.

While the visit to the nonprofit event was a triumph, things were not all good. By this point in the summer everyone was politely ignoring the fact that surviving the school year as an emotional support for so many people had basically ruined me. My anxiety was out of control; I wasn't sleeping and I was struggling to do simple tasks like return phone calls or check my email. Esther and I began a morning routine of waking up well before the fiery Vegas sun was up and getting at least a four mile run in. Sometimes we ran trails around the base of the mountain and sometimes we found ourselves touring the golf course and retirement community nearby. On more than one occasion we got lost and had to google map our way home. On days when I woke up with crippling anxiety we would stay close to home endlessly circling our block before the sun came up, me listening to a series of podcasts and Esther quivering with excitement just to be outside. We would return home sweaty and breathless and Esther would immediately charge straight into the pool and swim a lap before climbing onto the kid's trampoline and jumping by herself until she was dry. Now I look fondly back on those early mornings alone with my dog, but in the moment it felt like the exercise equivalent of thumb sucking. I knew I needed to calm down and get my emotions regulated, but I just didn't know how.

Zack struggled to figure out how to be appropriately supportive. He was used to seeing me take charge of situations and people, more often a bull in a china shop than anything else. Now he would find me sitting in front of a closed laptop in tears, unable to make myself open it up and read through the day's emails. I began to get offended at social invitations from friends. Even a text message suggesting that we meet for dinner felt like one more person making demands on me. I shrunk my world down until it included only my husband, children, and my three closest friends. Typically immensely social, I stopped returning even text messages and did everything I could to avoid interacting with anyone else. At the time it didn't feel out of the ordinary. I justified it as "self-care," the magical phrase all counselors are taught and something that can be called on like an automatic excuse to take a bubble bath or avoid something you dread. I like to think that I am a good counselor and that I am intuitive and insightful with others. With myself, apparently, I need some work because I wasn't able to put together that this kind of isolation would only make me more phobic.

My husband gently, and then not so gently, suggested that I find a counselor of my own to talk to. I am used to being on the receiving end of

people looking for therapists and have compiled a list of fantastic profes-
sionals over the years. I'm proud of my referral list and confident in everyone on there. When it came to finding someone for myself I simply couldn't
manage. I didn't want to see anyone on my list and wind up compromising
a professional relationship or putting them in an awkward position because
they knew me as a peer or as a referral source. I couldn't blindly pick someone off of the internet and risk not being able to trust their professional
discretion. Navigating our insurance was overwhelming and felt impossible.
I procrastinated for weeks, alternately googling online therapy programs or
trying to convince myself I was fine. The whole experience was incredibly
humbling and I am grateful for it, as I think it has made me more gracious
and mindful when I am assisting others in finding help.

Eventually I found a counselor, a humorless man who specialized in
cognitive behavioral therapy. I appreciated him because he didn't waste time
explaining things that I already knew and sent me off with homework after
every session to expedite the process. I don't know if he was that good of a
counselor or if I was just so relieved to finally feel empowered again, but I
started feeling better pretty quickly. It started to feel like maybe it would all
pass and things would be ok.

Even more than therapy, more than the crack of dawn runs, more than
the time with my dog, the biggest help during that summer came from my
three best friends, the dance moms. Haley, Kimmy, Amber and I had grown
incredibly close over the last year while surviving dance competitions and
hauling our kids around. I've always done community well, especially with
Zack's job sporadically changing his schedule while I've been working full
time. I'm good at trading kids back and forth and helping each other out.
In another life I would've killed it living on a commune. While I've done
community well, I have never done intimacy well. I tend to fix other people
and hold my own stuff in, sometimes embarrassed by how important it is
to me to give the appearance that I have it all together. I think a lot of us
are wired this way, to unintentionally martyr ourselves in friendships and
always be the one to save the day or refuse to be vulnerable for whatever
reason. While it feels great to be the one that everyone goes to, that isn't
authentic friendship. I really didn't realize until this stressful summer that
I was treating almost everyone in my life like they were either potential or
current counseling clients. This realization helped explain why I was getting irate at every social invitation; every time someone reached out to me
I assumed they wanted support for something for themselves because that's
what I was used to giving.

My friendship with these three was different in a way that I couldn't
explain. Maybe it was the fateful cat peeing on me incident that sealed the

deal, maybe it was the number of times they had watched me unsuccessfully try to glue fake eyelashes on my daughter while she fought me like a barn cat, maybe it was all those dance competitions where I wandered in sherpa'ing a hundred pounds of rhintestoned costumes and not nearly enough snacks on my own because Zack had been called into work again. Whatever it was I was finally truly vulnerable in friendship for the first time in my adult life. And these women continued to rally, with a barrage of benign text conversations, showing up for breakfasts and mornings runs, and organizing family events. They forced me to stay in the rhythm of life in a time when I wanted to spiral and stop trying.

Chapter 14

When Humbled is the Place to Be

TIME AT BRAD CAMP taught Esther to really love two things: swimming and going down playground slides. He told me when we first started with training that one of the best things to do with new puppies was to take them to playgrounds and teach them go down the slides. It's a scary thing for them, but once they are coaxed down they realize how much fun it is which plants the idea that when I ask her to do things she is unsure of she can trust me that it will be ok.

And wow, did Esther take to the slide.

To the point that she is now almost three years old and still quivers with excitement when we pass a playground. If I take her leash off and let her go she will spend a good half an hour racing up the steps and zinging down the slide with her tongue flapping in the wind. I have to make sure to grab her right away if kids show up to play because she is just not good at waiting her turn. Her round orange bottom will bump kids right out of the way as she cuts to the front of the line every time. She may be popular at school, but she is kind of a menace on the playground. In fact, we may actually be on some kind of playground watch list.

Even more than the slides, Brad taught Esther to love to swim. We've never had a dog that swam before and initially it was such novel fun to see her go flying off the side to splash after a ball or to slip onto the wet deck to cool herself off. She is not graceful in the least but it is adorable to see her little sausage dog body go sailing into the water.

Soon her routine evolved to include sliding onto the wet deck for one slow lap around the pool every time she returned from a walk. Then it became common for her to want to slip in for a quick dip after any kind of fetch or activity. The novelty of it all started to wear off when she began taking a lap every time she was let outside.

"No swimming!" we would sternly remind her before opening the back door.

"Swimming." her eyes responded every time, her mind already made up.

We would open the door and she would nonchalantly wander into the yard. Maintaining eye contact with whoever had let her out she would slowly immerse herself like curly loch ness monster, taking one deliberate lap while defiantly staring us down. On more than one occasion I would find Zack shaking a fist at the yard like an old man while a wet dog rocketed through the dirt in the planters. I thought it was funny until the time came for Esther and I to report back to work in August. I would let her out in the morning one last time before we had to leave and she would turn up at the door soaking wet just seconds later.

'She's a magician? I don't get it? She can be on the trampoline and if you turn around for a split second she's somehow in the deep end?" Zack was at his wit's end.

As much as Esther enjoys going to work, she also really enjoys finding ways to get out of work. I couldn't risk her realizing that if she was soaked from swimming I would put the vest away and she could stay home. So, on more occasions than I like to admit I loaded that wet mess into my car and hauled her into work. Thankfully we were able to break her of the habit (mostly) in the weeks before the kids were back on campus, so it was only staff who had to endure the stink of wet dog in back to school meetings or who would reach to pet her only to snatch a hand back from the wet mop. This was the start of Esther's first full year of employment, so showing up with her like this was very humbling indeed.

Looking back I can see that all of the animal uprisings, the pink eye, the unruly leash behavior and slide dominance, the utter loss of control over my anxiety and most aspects of my life all worked together to land me in a place where I clearly had not spent enough time; the valley of totally humbled. There is a curious kind of relief that comes with being utterly broken. My husband is fond of the saying that there are no atheists in foxholes, after a long career as a first responder he has lived a lifetime of seeing people in their very worst moments. When he worked as a patrol cop, he made it a habit to keep the Christian fish visible in his police car at all times and had many long conversations about Jesus with people who were struggling. God sure does use those valleys in life to humble us and rope us in closer to him, no matter how hard we may fight against it.

We see dear Queen Esther facing a similar kind of brokenness and valley of humility as she readies herself to face the king. I've always wondered if during those three long days of fasting and prayer she seriously considered backing out. She didn't have to get scared and humble and risk everything. Esther entirely had the option of turning a blind eye and saving her own skin. She could have remained comfortably the queen and lived out all of her days basically doing whatever she wanted as long as it didn't upset the king. I imagine that while there was no part of her that would peacefully accept the idea of her cousin and all of her people being murdered, I'm sure some of the thoughts had to swirl in her head that we all have when faced with something terrifying.

'It'll probably be fine."

"There's no way (insert disaster) could actually happen."

"There is nothing special enough about me to take on (huge monumental impending doom)."

And my personal favorite excuse to avoid something I am afraid of:

"There has to be someone, someone who is better at things than me, who will step up and take care of this."

It's in the moments of fear, self-doubt, and a dash of self-loathing that God most often draws us close and fills us with courage. It's not until we are humbled are we ready to receive that courage. Esther was queen of the land, and while she was not immune to the whims of the king and came nowhere close to having his power she certainly had her own authority that she had become used to wielding. Once she had resolved herself to help it would have been horribly humanly easy to attempt to use that power. Esther could have made herself extra beautiful, covered herself in expensive jewels and robes, and marched into the king's chambers attempting to use both her beauty and her power as queen.

She could have been arrogant. She could have believed that her wealth or her political power would carry her through. And while the book of Esther does not outright mention God by name, we see her clearly getting very still and choosing to rely on Him. This humility saved her and her people.

By contrast, Haman's refusal to be humbled is what started everything in motion. Throughout the book he is presented with opportunities to act in humility, which he rejects every time. Not to spoil an ending but Haman himself winds up hanging from the very gallows he constructed for Mordecai. His grudge began when his ego refused to accept the fact that Mordecai would not bow to him. This grudge extended beyond Mordecai to all of the Jews for a few reasons, one being that Haman was descended from the Amalekites who were ancient enemies of the Jewish people. Even more than a historical grudge, Haman could not stomach that the Jewish people as a race refused to see him as a final authority figure. The man could not bear the thought that the Jews would disregard his power in favor of God. It intensified when he was forced to honor Mordecai for his role in thwarting the murder plot against Xerxes.

Haman also makes an error that is so sinfully human, one that we are all guilty of. Once he realizes that he doesn't like Mordecai, he starts working on recruiting others to not like him as well. Granted, his audience was a king. Yet how often do we find ourselves defensive about someone and so we seek to gain some assurance by enlisting others to join our cause. Now we are all adults here, good Christian people, so we would never do anything as sinful as trying to enlist others in actively disliking someone. Instead we hide behind the curtains of "venting," "advice seeking," and "let me run this by you." They all have the same goal, we want our egos reassured that we are right, we are liked, we are valuable, and that others are willing to take up our cause.

Before you think I am getting judgy and preachy, let me convict myself as Example A out on the front lawn of this kind of behavior. Insecurity drives us to seek approval, even when it is at the expense of others.

Haman sidled himself up to the king, most likely with a drink in hand, and began his campaign under the guise of "oh boy, you should really know about these people who are out to get you." Conveniently leaving out any mention of his own personal feelings, Haman weaves a tale for the king of an untrustworthy group living among them who are prepared to defy the king's power at every time. Reassured that he is the king's best boy, Haman gets the go ahead for his murder plot. This still isn't enough for Haman's ego. The book of Esther tells us that he is enraged after this when he sees Mordecai and Mordecai still isn't visibly afraid of him.

The same way I wonder about Queen Esther's thoughts racing in those days leading up to approaching the king, I also wonder about Haman's thoughts when the hangman's mask and noose were placed on him. Did he regret caring so much about the perceived slight when Mordecai would not bow? Did he see the waste of energy and the hatred he spewed as he turned the king against an entire people? As he feared the end of his own life, did he have a second to ruminate on why he had felt it was so important for people to fear him? Was he able to grasp that a few moments of humility would have potentially righted this whole ship?

Perhaps most of all, did he find that it is true that there are no atheists in foxholes? Facing his own death, did he have a moment to consider the God that the Jews knew to be the final authority?

Chapter 15

Comforting the Shaken. . .

Try Not to Make it Weird

A COMFORT DOG, WHILE amazing, is still "just" a dog. Starting a canine program in a school is exciting, but it typically does not change the world. What does change the world is when we find ways to truly comfort the people around us. It is when we are in our darkest times and the horror of the world has overwhelmed us that we are called to be helpers and to do whatever we can to counter the horror facing us. Those of us still standing are to care for the hurt. This is a big calling, but also the best way I know to get through these scary times. Bonus points if you can do the work and maintain joy and contentment, something I am still working on.

Why God allows evil in the world is an age old question, posed by school children and preached from pulpits. Sin is evil, the world is full of sin, this side of heaven we will not know the truest peace and joy. All of this doesn't mean that God isn't in control, but it can make things feel awfully bleak. Whenever tragedy strikes it is inevitable that our social media feeds fill with thoughts and prayers and someone always posts the quote attributed to Mr. Rogers, to look for the helpers. That someone who posts that quote is usually me. In the times that we are the most hurt by other people, looking for the people who are doing good helps to combat that hopelessness. Being one of the people doing good feels like taking back power in a powerless situation, although it can be difficult to know exactly what kind of good to do.

It is so hard to know what to say when someone you love is suffering. It's also hard when someone you only kind of know but really like is suffering. And it is really hard and awkward when someone you don't know well or maybe have a history of conflict with is suffering.

Oftentimes we don't know what to do and so we just make it weird.

We cave into the pressure of feeling as though we need to speak on God's behalf and we spout the kind of Christian comfort found on flowery greeting cards. Or we get even weirder and start avoiding the person in need. We misfire words of encouragement that are received as dismissive.

In the year following 1 October, our school suffered unspeakable losses within our faculty's families and within our student body. These tragedies were unrelated to the mass shooting, yet it just felt as though death surrounded us and each day brought about more horrific news. As we returned to campus for the 2018/19 school year we were faced with the loss of another child. A brilliant and beautiful student passed away following a lengthy illness, leaving our community shaken once again. I was called upon to write a statement and devotion for our faculty and I was at a loss. Gathering our entire faculty to absorb more tragedy and then shore everyone up to serve our students was happening all too often and I was running out of ways to verbalize hope and comfort.

I paged through Romans and Philippians, thinking that no one knew more about suffering than my hero, the Apostle Paul. Paul was the kind of guy who could take a literal beating, be thrown into a dungeon hole, and somehow make friends with the guards and get them to send out the letters of encouragement he wrote to groups of believers who were in arguably better circumstances than him.

He also began his story as an incredibly violent man, hell bent on murdering Christians and putting a stop to the growth of the early Christian church. An encounter with Jesus flipped his life on its axis and turned him into a fearless preacher and author of somewhere between eight and thirteen books of the New Testament, depending on which scholars you believe. Paul is proof that our beginnings don't have to be our whole story and that God can change and use anyone.

Paul is also the original content in any circumstances kind of guy. I'm pretty sure he was one of the people whose simple presence just made everyone feel better. I'd love to be like Paul, calm and encouraging, quietly trusting God and taking joy in Him, a reassuring presence to all who are suffering.

Instead, I poured a glass of wine and wept over the New Testament while I wrote and deleted the same sentence over and over. Eventually I gave up and called Katie Wiltse, a former theology teacher at our school and hands down one of the most naturally joyful and humble people I know. While I fail constantly in so many ways, I do excel at realizing that I am surrounded by incredibly intelligent and resourceful people and that I need to take advantage of that community. Katie had already heard the bad news of our recent loss and sympathized as I shared my struggle to find a way to offer some type of condolence.

"I'm all over the Epistles. Paul was writing from a mud pit and was able to get the job done. I still can't find anything to say."

I'll never forget Katie's response.

"Oh, girl. You gotta take this one back to Job."

In the Old Testament, poor Job suffered more than any man before or after him, losing all of his children, all of his worldly possessions, and eventually falling ill and being covered in painful sores. We may have hard days, but to have your children perish, your financial security completely erased, and then be covered in weeping sores so painful that you can't even sit comfortably? That is a seriously bad day. Once a wealthy patriarch of a powerful family, Job wound up sitting along the side of the road in a pile of ashes scraping at his sores with bits of broken pottery.

For real. The Bible takes care to point out that Job was actually sitting in a dust pile scratching at oozing wounds with bits of broken bowls, possible even remnants of his former posh life. His wife is so disgusted by all of it that she is quoted as asking Job why he doesn't give up his integrity, curse God, and just go die. The footnote on this is interesting; some scholars speculate that the reason Job's wife was spared after the rest of the family perished was because her very presence caused him even more anguish.

Note to self, when your loved ones are suffering at least try to not cause more anguish. Or at least try not to be THAT wife.

Job's three best friends rolled up to this sorry state of affairs determined to offer some support. Eliphaz, Bildad, and Zophar loved Job dearly and watched him suffer to a degree that few humans will ever experience. We've all had friends mourn the death of a loved one, flounder financially, have marriages end, or be faced with health issues. It can be a struggle to know how to comfort in those times. Chapter two of Job sees his friends kind of getting their roles of comforters right; they showed up to be with him, sympathized with him, and spent time with him. In Job 2:11–13 we see that they were by his side for seven full days, weeping and tearing their own robes.

This silent sitting is a part of Jewish tradition and one that probably needs to be brought back into modern times. Tradition stated that when people come to comfort someone in mourning, they were to sit silently and wait until the mourner speaks. There is such wisdom in this silent presence, allowing feelings to flow and to support with loving calm. They wept with him and mourned with him, but for a full week did not break silence with awkward prose or explanation. There were probably some whispered side conversations on trips to the bathroom or to get snacks, the kind that happens among friends when you are seriously worried about the sanity and well-being of one of your own. But then? Straight back to no words, just weeping and tearing robes along with their buddy Job.

I have to give these guys some credit here, while I have comforted many people in my career I have never upped my comfort game to a robe tearing level.

But after seven days of comforting in silence, Job's buddies could not be silent any longer and here is where they got everything wrong. While they still loved Job and wanted to see his suffering end, they started desperately reaching for reasons why he was suffering and eventually drew the condemnation of God. Each in his own way tried to talk Job around to taking the blame for his suffering, that his own sin had in some way brought all of this tragedy upon him. While much of the speeches they offered up are easily dismissed by us today, how often do we fall into the trap of trying to make sense of tragedy in an attempt to comfort a friend? And how often are we guilty of just avoiding those in hurt because we have run out of comforting words to offer? My heart broke when a co-worker once told me that after his cancer diagnosis became public he felt like a dead man walking, not from the cancer but from the way people avoided him to avoid the topic.

I've heard many grieving or traumatized people repeat in disbelief some of the well intended statements made by loved ones. And best believe I've done plenty of fumbling around myself trying to find the right words in hard situations. Relationships get weird when people just don't know what to say.

We fall into the greatest traps when we feel like we have to explain things for God. Even though we know that people don't hurt on earth as a punishment for shortcomings and we also know that God's plans are bigger and more complex than we could ever hope to explain, we still succumb to the pressure of trying to find an explanation or make things right. This will usually make us start saying the kind of cheesy statements found on cheap sympathy cards, which can be so deeply wounding to the person grieving.

So how do we help those that hurt? The brilliant Apostle Paul tells us in Romans 12:15 that we should "mourn with those who mourn." We should sit with those who hurt, acknowledge their pain, be prepared to admit that we have no idea what God's plan is, and continually turn the focus back to the greatest comforter, our heavenly Father. We should also be ready for whatever doors open in the healing process.

Maybe we can draw the line at robe tearing for the sake of empathy, but there is always the chance to find a way to be the light in dark times. Maybe starting a school dog program isn't always appropriate (although I bet it usually is). When faced with darkness and hurting people, all we can do is love hard and try not to make it weird.

Chapter 16

Except That Sometimes it is Going to Get Weird

WHEN I WAS PREGNANT with my kids I invariably found myself in the same exam room at nearly every visit to the doctor. My ob-gyn had hung a poster declaring "Live Like Someone Left the Gate Open" with the picture of a small fluffy dog in mid-flight. Because Petey was almost two weeks overdue, this left me with a lot of extra time to consider this sentiment and also wonder why it had been chosen to inspire those of us who were busy heaving around extra weight and growing eyelashes for people other than ourselves.

Petey is now almost a teenager and has a unique bond to Esther. It is a blend of sincere love and the little bit of the sibling rivalry that comes with having a somewhat famous younger sister. Kids are always telling Petey that she is so lucky to live with Esther. While Esther can usually hold it together in public, it can be quite a different story at home. When she isn't digging up sprinklers or chasing the cat she enjoys swimming and jumping on the trampoline. She will jump by herself, which is charming, but she really enjoys jumping with the kids. That has always delighted me. Whenever Petey has friends over and they go outside to jump I encourage them to take the little orange furball with them. I'll watch them all jumping from the kitchen window and silently congratulate myself on the idyllic childhood I've provided for my kids. Puppies, swimming, a trampoline? I'm basically the best mom ever. The kids really need to thank me more often.

One beautiful night Petey was outside laying on the trampoline. It was that awesome time in Vegas when the sun is just going down, it isn't surface of the sun hot, but the air is still nice and warm. A breeze was gently blowing as I decided to go and join her. Being in my 40s and having birthed two children, the trampoline isn't typically my jam. I figured as long as we were just laying quietly and not jumping I could get by without, erm, incident. All of you moms know what I mean. The rest of you? Don't worry about it.

We laid quietly side by side enjoying the night and talking about the week ahead. As we chatted, Evan opened up the back door and let Esther out. She cruised around the yard for a few seconds and I listened to her snuffling in the bushes. Suddenly, her face appeared at the side of the trampoline net by the zipper closing us in.

"I'm ready for you." Petey muttered through gritted teeth.

Before I could grasp what was happening, Esther stuck her nose under the zipper and jerked the net open. She launched herself onto the trampoline, paws outstretched in what I quickly discovered was a Superman punch headed directly for my groin. I flashed back to the happy dog midflight on the OB's wall as her 45lbs of service dog trained fury landed on top of me. I rolled to my side, wind knocked out of me, as she began jumping on my head. While I was battling my way to my feet Petey was already up on hers, swaying side to side in a move that I once saw a trained Capoeira group perform in a mixed martial arts expo.

"YOU WANT SOME OF THIS?" she taunted the dog as Esther leaped at her and punched her in the neck. The dog repeatedly bounced off of the trampoline, shooting up to eye level before delivering expert kicks. If a kangaroo, Chuck Norris, and Snuffleupagus somehow combined DNA, this would be the result.

"What is happening?! Why is she doing this? Is it always like this?" I huddled against the net as Petey dodged blows from fluffy orange paws.

The sound of my voice reminded Esther of my presence and she began chasing me around the perimeter of the trampoline, launching herself at the back of my legs. I knew if she got me on the ground it was all over, but I also knew that if I fell full weight against the net I would go tumbling onto the decorative brick. I weighed my odds as I leapt/ran around the trampoline.

"Oh yeah, it's Fight Club out here," Petey wiped sweaty hair out of her eyes and adjusted her glasses. "Welcome to the Thunderdome." She turned and faced the dog, feet planted in a power pose. I am not too proud to admit that I actually hid behind her like the coward that I am. Fists clenched, she let out a war cry. Esther turned tail, launched herself from the trampoline, and began zooming around the yard.

"Petey. . . . ." I run half marathons routinely and I still struggled to catch my breath. "Is it seriously always like this? I thought you guys were out here having fun with her?"

Like a well-trained soldier, Petey kept one eye on the curly dog who was now attacking a pool float while she assured me that yes, yes, it is always like this.

I wiped dog spit off the back of my calves. "But. . .. I've sent your friends out here to jump with her. I've put her in the yard and encouraged this. I thought it was fun?"

Petey shrugged. "I can take a hit now. Get ready, she's coming for us."

When I looked up I could see the streak of orange beginning to rocket around the yard heading for the trampoline. I turned to my 12 year old for guidance on what to do. She told me we should run for it and so we did, barely making it to the door before the dog. Kind of like Cujo, except with punching instead of biting.

I seriously had no idea this was happening.

I probably owe some kids and their parents apologies.

We caught our breath inside and looked out to see Esther waiting on the side of the trampoline. Eventually she joined us in the house, curling up for snuggles like normal and apparently forgetting about the fight club we had been through earlier.

The next day I put her service vest back on her and we headed out, the world at large none the wiser to the terror she induces at home. She sat politely at work and waited for kids to pet her. Not once did she attempt to punch anyone in the groin. When the work day was over she came home and took herself back to the trampoline for some jumping.

And really, it's exactly how I pictured it would be when I first imagined a therapy dog program: a dog who is perfectly well behaved and serving a vital purpose by day and free to be a total trampoline jumping-kicking-superman punching-weirdo when the work day is over. You know, like the rest of us.

Chapter 17

Patience Means Wait Your Turn

WHEN MY DAUGHTER WAS little we had the good fortune of sending her to an in home preschool let by a beautiful soul named Ms. Monica. If there was to ever be a patron saint of patience, it would be Ms. Monica. She was patient through Petey's snack hoarding phase. She was patient through having a herd of two year old girls in the house. By the way, a herd of two year old girls is actually called a murder. You can trust me on that, I've done all of the research. Most of all, Ms. Monica was patient even through the terrifying time when my mother gifted Petey a frightening vintage doll that she named Angel Baby. Under the guise of family heirloom, I couldn't get away with destroying this hell minion and Petey took to it like it was a beautiful princess doll. She also took to hiding that creeper around Ms. Monica's house to surprise her.

With a dirty lace bonnet, maniacal eyes, and a sparse crop of red hair Angel Baby was the toy of nightmares. At the age of two Petey somehow had the determination and stealth hiding skills of a CIA agent in pull ups, who was tasked with planting surveillance bugs in mafia homes. Poor Ms. Monica. She didn't have a chance. The dear lady would open the bathroom door and find the face of an old timey clown baby leering around the shower curtain at her. Or she would open the snack cabinet to find a bonneted head and grimy orange curls poking out from between graham cracker boxes. Even worse were the times that Petey would manage to sneak Angel Baby into Ms. Monica's bedroom, tucking her under pillows on the bed to be discovered later that night or hiding her in a drawer under folded t-shirts to be discovered early one morning. No matter how hard I tried to protect Ms. Monica from Angel Baby, Petey would always find ways to sneak that horrible doll into her house. It would have completely broken a lesser woman.

Ms. Monica also managed to stay patient each time a new backyard toy was delivered and her entire murder of two year olds had to learn to take turns on whatever the shiny new apparatus was. She diffused the entire bunch with the catch phrase she taught them.

"Patience means wait your turn!" Petey would chant this at us so often that I eventually had to make it a point to thank Ms. Monica for introducing it, even if it meant that I now had to stand in line every family dinner until Petey gifted me a napkin and silverware and I also had to jockey for a spot in line to use the bathroom. Run by a dictator toddler, order ruled our house in those times as we all patiently waited our turn. I'm forever grateful that Petey had Ms. Monica teaching her about patience and self-control at such a young age, although I still don't know how she survived the reign of Angel Baby.

Waiting and self-control are just such hard things to master. They are even harder when we are under direct stress or feeling that things have spun completely out of our control. We've all felt stress, but few of us have felt the pressure to save our entire people from genocide kind of stress.

We left things at an awkward time with Queen Esther and the city of Susa. Haman had convinced the King to eradicate the Jews, Mordecai had gone into mourning and then convinced Esther she had to be very brave, her people were fasting and praying with her for guidance. While the ending may be spoiled and we all know that eventually Haman reaped what he sowed, we can't miss the opportunity to go through all of the delicious twists and turns that lead to such a huge climax.

After three days of fasting and praying, Esther dusted herself off and donned her royal robes. Here is another trait of hers that I have long admired; her ability to avoid the extreme thinking that we should either do nothing but pray or behave as though everything is up to us. This thinking is so tempting, we either get a free pass to just hand it to God or we get the ego trip that we are actually in control. There is an often quoted old adage that makes sense of this, reminding us that we are to pray as everything depends on God but work as if everything depends on us. God works through the people who are willing to act for Him. What a contradictory tension to live in! Yet here we have Esther, living out one of only two books of the Bible to never mention God, demonstrating exactly this. God doesn't appear in a burning bush to tell her what to do. Esther doesn't get to march up a mountain and receive direct reassurance that God has her back. This is so inspiring for those of us alive today who must fix our faith on the unseen yet unchanging God. Queen Esther set the example for us by focusing in prayer and then being prepared to work when it was time to act.

Shored up and in this new state of action, Esther prepared herself to face her king. I have to imagine it was a lot like when you emerge from a few days in bed following an illness or tragedy and put on some mascara, pull up your big girl panties, and steady yourself to face what's next. And oh, but the drama that is about to unfold!

Esther, dressed to impress, approached the king's hallway and was met with a glad reception by him. For all of his faults, Xerxes really did adore Queen Esther. He told her that whatever she wanted, up to half of the entire kingdom, could be hers for the asking. She responded that all she wanted was for the king and his buddy Haman to come to a banquet that she had prepared for them. That's it. The king responded by summoning Haman from whatever evil business he was up to and the three of them settled in for some wine and good food. During this feast, Xerxes had the presence of mind to ask Esther again what she was seeking when she came to his court. She replied that she would like the two of them to come to another banquet the following night. As mentioned earlier, the night of this first banquet was the evening when the king could not sleep and so had the royal records read to him, leading to Haman having interrupt his building of gallows to parade Mordecai about town. Talk about timing!

Even more impressive than the timing is Esther's sheer self-control throughout this day. A long running joke in my marriage is that Zack can witness {insert any horrible event} during the course of his work day and calmly come home to family dinner. Weeks or even months later he will casually mention said horrible event and what he witnessed and then continue to go about his business. I'm married to the greatest master of compartmentalizing who ever lived. I operate in a different mode with him and have been known to be waiting in the garage as he pulls in just so I can tell him that someone raised their voice at me. I just can't hold it in with him. A particularly tumultuous day for me means that he will find himself hostage on a four mile walk while I use 3.75 of those miles to work through whatever conflict I faced. The hardest of days means that he will have to endure the walk and also me trying to continue the conversation with him through a door while he's in the shower after.

He's very patient.

He is also accepting sympathy cards.

If I were in Esther's shoes I would not have had the patience and self-control to slow play this out. Not one bit. The very first time I showed up in front of Xerxes that morning and he said I could have whatever I wanted, up to half the kingdom, I would have been a hysterical snot snobbing mess, weeping and dramatically pointing at Haman while I rambled all over about the evil that was afoot. It would not have been pretty and certainly no one would have ever described it as regal.

If we are all being painfully honest, how many of us could have acted with this kind of self-control? The extremes would have been much more appealing. On one hand, we could just "give it to God" and go through the motions of praying and waiting for someone else to step up. When the genocide eventually occurred, we could tell ourselves it was God's plan and go to bed in our Queenly chambers. Even more appealing would have been to head over to the other extreme upon hearing Haman's plan and to march directly into the king's chambers tattling on everyone involved.

I really think if I were in Esther's shoes I would have done the 480 B.C. equivalent of waiting in the garage for my husband. I would have paced around, entirely unpeaceful, and eventually hunted him down to unload all of the ways that I thought I had been wronged and all of my solutions for fixing the injustices. I would have been emotional and unhinged by the unfairness of it all. I would not have had the good old Ms. Monica patience to wait my turn.

The difference is that when I act like this now I am met with veiled sighs and agreement to take a long walk by a long suffering man who not only adores me but treats me as a partner in life. Were Esther to have behaved in this irrational fashion she most likely would have found herself relieved of her Queenly duties at a minimum.

Patience means wait your turn. Surrendering everything to God and being prepared to get to work when the time is right. His time, not our time.

Chapter 18

Even Comfort Dogs Get the Blues

ONE FALL DAY I was faced with a remarkably distressing dilemma. Namely, I really needed a coffee, had to buy some flowers, and I had a dog with me. Esther had just turned a year old. She was a totally different dog than she was six months earlier, but I was still sometimes hesitant with her. She isn't a service dog, she is a comfort dog, and although she wears a vest she does not get to have access to all of the places that a service dog does. I've learned that two topics are very polarizing in the working dog community: purchasing from a breeder vs adopting and those who take liberties with a dog in a vest to gain access to places that are not dog friendly. There is a big difference between a dog who needs to remain with a person to prevent medical episodes or assist with mobility and a Comfort Dog.

Even if I was inclined to push the rules, which I am not, Esther is not always one hundred percent on her best behavior. Which leads us to a cold November morning with Esther, Petey, and I standing outside of the grocery store across the street from school. I desperately needed to run in and get flowers for one of our rockstar kids who was signing that day to play college ball. Basic as we are, Petey and I both desperately needed a hot drink from the coffee shop inside the store. Neither of us were sure what to do with Esther, who may or may not eat the seats in my new Jeep if left unattended. Also, see above about needing to follow rules. So, no dogs left in cars. Not even with child chaperones.

"I don't know. Maybe I'll drop you and Esther at school and run back here. But then I'll be late for work." I stewed out loud. Petey shifted her weight from foot to foot.

"No, it's fine. She's pretty well trained. I won't let her touch anything. She has the vest on. I really want a coffee. . .. . .." I trailed off while Esther stared up at me.

"But she's not a SERVICE service dog and all of the people with service dogs get so mad when dogs like this go into places that only allow service dogs." Petey sighed loudly and started scrolling through her phone.

"Let's just go for it," I told her. "You get coffee and I'll go straight to the flowers with the dog and not let her near any food. I'll meet you at the entrance." We shook on it, I gave her some money, and Esther perked up a little in her red working vest.

As I nervously ushered dog and child inside I heard an audible shriek and saw one of the store employees sprinting toward us. I braced myself for a good shaming about bringing dogs where they don't belong. Truth be told, I tried to quickly figure out if I could outrun her if I fled to my car and left Petey stranded. She could find her way to school, right? The three inch heels I was sporting and my fear that Esther would somehow clothesline me with her leash kept me in my place.

"Is that Esther? Is that the dog from the news? Are we allowed to pet her?" The lady was a little winded from her jog and paused with her fingers stretched toward the dog. I told her that Esther would love a good pet. She bent over and began running her fingers through Esther's fluff.

"I've been having such a hard day." She suddenly crumbled to her knees, hugging the dog tightly. Esther did what Esther does and leaned against the woman, absorbing her tears and getting very still. I awkwardly patted at them both, because Esther is much better at impromptu comfort than I am. After a few moments the lady dried her tears, stood up, thanked me, and went back to her checkout station. I could hear her telling the other employees about Esther.

I looked down at the dog. She looked up at me from under her mop of hair. She seemed once again extra smug, like she had been telling me all along that she could handle going to the grocery store and I should just trust her.

'You probably think you deserve a new toy, don't you?" Esther nodded and we ventured a little deeper into the grocery store to pick out something that she would ultimately end up violently disemboweling on my office floor even before lunchtime.

Later that month I was sitting at my desk answering an endless stream of emails early one morning. Esther, resigned to being at work, was snoring gently in her kennel in the corner of my office. The peace was broken by the arrival of my high school principal, Scott, who was agitated about an issue. Usually incredibly affable and good natured, now he loomed in my doorway on the verge of ranting with frustration. A little orange head emerged from the kennel and Esther scooted over to him to bury her face in his knees. Scott continued to vent, but his tone gradually got lighter as he continued to pet her head while he finished his story.

Eventually he just laughed, "Ok, you got me. You did it. I'm comforted. I do feel better, Esther."

Appearing to understand that her work here was done, Esther turned and headed back to her kennel to resume her important business of napping and chewing on her vest when she thought I wasn't looking. I hid a smile as Scott left for a meeting. The dog typically doesn't give him the time of day, unless he has a toy and is trying to get her riled up. She tends to blow right by both Dan and Scott, to their frustration, but I have always chalked it up to her knowledge that neither of them requires much by way of comfort. She really amazes me with her intuition in knowing when people, even the normally well adjusted, need a little extra love.

The constant juggling of emotion can be wearing on everyone. Compassion fatigue is real, yo. While I am hippy dippy to the point of making my own deodorant and putting it on every morning with the back of a spoon to the utter disgust of my husband, I do have to brace myself whenever I head off to a conference for counselors. They can take things to the next level. Like education, the counseling world tends to spin in cycles of buzz words and trends. Only instead of "differentiated instruction" or "project based learning" we use things like "empowering bystanders" and "cultures of reporting." I guess it's normal, but whenever you get together a group of people who absorb the problems of others for a living, things can quickly turn into a forum for offloading stress and emotion which we cleverly disguise as "self-care" strands.

The term self-care is so overwrought in the counseling community that I once spent an entire weekend mentally taking a shot every time the phrase was spoken or written. We learned about Epsom salt baths, the importance of saying no, the dedicated practice of mindful meditation, and something about closing your door when the day gets too stressful. While that sounds reasonable, it is not a practice I've never been able to master because bodies tend to pile up in the hall outside of my office like a Civil War battle when I try it.

Snarky as I can be about it, the practices of mindfulness, stillness, prayer, exercise, and getting centered are just so essential. I do understand that. It's the old axiom that if the plane is going down we need to place the oxygen mask on ourselves before we can save those around us.

It can be hard to not allow those important self-care practices to become just another stressful thing on the long and busy to do list.

Went running while obsessing over a hitch in the school schedule? Check.

Sat stewing in a luke-warm bath of Epsom salt and lavender while replaying a hard conversation in my head? Check.

Threw myself through a rage yoga practice that I don't really remember, but can count it as time on my mat? Check.

How about that prayer journal that reads like one part critical yelp review and one part wish list for a magic genie? Got it. All set. That's mine. Good to go.

Check, check, check.

Even worse than the half-hearted attempts to cross self-care activities off of my daily habit checklist is the total guilt that comes with not checking them off at all. How utterly boring and human to be stressed and full of self-hatred for not completing the very things meant to make us feel less stressed and more self-accepting?

Compassion fatigue tags along behind self-care, the unspoken fall out of refusing bubble baths, skipping morning exercise, and resisting all effort to silence the shame voice in our head that reminds us we are failing. I think every mental health worker has found themselves deep in the grips of compassion fatigue at one point or another. It's the moment when you find yourself unable to drum up the appropriate emotional engagement for whatever is being shared with you. My work husband, Dan, and I joke that it is just being dead inside and it is a quality that makes for a great non-reactive counselor. It's the thing that allows us to sit together and talk about the worst phone calls we've ever had to make, stories of death and sexual assault, and then decide that we need to go get fresh cups of coffee. I see it with my husband and our first responder friends, the compartmentalizing and shutting down that lets you get up and face each day.

The tricky part, as a counselor or caregiver, is when you are in the depths of fatigue and the problems keep rolling in. I can do crisis all day long, but having to down shift to trivial annoyances and then come back to crisis is the fastest way to render me useless. I cannot dredge the same level of care for someone not liking the way a PE teacher makes a student run laps that is needed for the loss of a grandparent. We are all only human, after all. What I didn't realize is that this isn't just a human condition, as Esther has proven to not be immune to it. While she will heave herself out of her kennel time and time again to provide some love and comfort for those in need, over a year into her work she started to show some serious discernment over who needed her comfort and what level of support they would receive from her.

One morning Esther and I had a busy start to the day. We had two different students grieving the loss of a family member and an adult struggling with heavy personal issues. Esther had just settled into her kennel for a deserved break and I was hunkering down to answer a slew of emails that I was grateful had not turned into phone calls. (Is there anything worse than a phone call that could have been an email?) Our quiet was interrupted by a highly strung student rocketing onto my couch. I love this kid. All emotion for this one is felt at a level 11. The highs are high, the lows are low, and there is a certain exhausting charm in seeing life through this lens of intensity. Over our years together we have developed a rhythm; when the day gets overwhelming the student comes in to offload and then is able to refocus and head back to class. The arrival of Esther took our counseling time together from an average of about fifteen minutes to well under ten. There is just something about that unkempt orange fur that always deescalates things quickly.

On this particular day Esther wasn't having it. The kid landed on my couch in a ball of theatrical sobs over the sheer degradation of having two points taken off of an assignment for turning it in late. I hid a smile behind my coffee cup, knowing that this was a small storm and we would be back on track in no time.

"It is NOT MY FAULT and I AM NEVER LATE and I should totally get a grace pass.....Esther.....ESTHER........ESTHERRRRRRR."

I looked down at the kennel. Esther's black bear nose had poked out of her hiding spot at the sound of her name, but she wasn't any closer to coming out.

"Esther?"

At this the dog heaved a deep sigh, the kind of sigh I heave when the message light on my phone is flashing menacingly, started to lift her head but then gave up and laid it back down.

I know that feeling. Oh Lord, do I know that feeling.

"Is she sick?" My kiddo's tears had dried up and been replaced with genuine concern for the dog.

"I think she's just tired. She's had a long morning. How about if you head to class and we sort all of this out a little later?" I knew full well the indignity of the two point loss would be forgotten by lunch.

Once the office was empty again I took Esther's tennis ball from its hiding spot and gave it a few bounces. Her fuzzy tank body flew out of that kennel with enough force to rock it side to side.

I knew it. Compassion fatigue. I'm totally drawing this dog an Epsom salt bath and pouring her a glass of wine when we get home.

Chapter 19

We are All a Little Traumatized Round Here

IN THE TIME FOLLOWING 1 October I've written enough and spoken enough that I can occasionally get taken seriously as a resource for working with youth who have been through horrific experiences. "Trauma informed practices" is the official educational tagline and it makes me sound smarter than I am. It is really a fancy way of saying "one way or another we are going to love these kids and get them to adulthood." Except no one would want to sign up for a conference with that title, partly because no one wants to hear about "one way or another." We all want neat little checklists, boxes that will result in success and healing if we just tick them off in order. It's human to want order and a clear path to success and that need is intensified among those of us who work with kids and who very much want to do right by them. If only grief and trauma would cooperate and be so linear and predictable.

When I speak to groups of educators and counselors they all stare at me expectantly, waiting for that magical healing checklist. Herding children through trauma recovery is heartbreaking work and there is always an air of desperation around those in the thick of it. I am devasted by those expectant stares. They pit my stomach with almost as much dread as the equally hopeful and helpless looks on the faces of parents of my traumatized kids.

It's the face of waiting for an answer that I just don't have. Because here is the best kept secret of the professional counselor: we have no idea. Of all of the counselors I've talked to over the years, we all can admit to the same moments. The ones where you are expected to have the answer and all you can do is hold the emotional barometer of the room to a steady hum and pray things unfold in a positive way. Why do you think one of the most comically common questions in therapy is "how does that make you feel?" We aren't looking for insight, we are buying time.

At the risk of extremely over simplifying a complicated profession, we let people talk and rephrase what they say back and ask questions until things become simple enough to untangle. The art of counseling is walking through another's brain and helping them to examine long held beliefs and personal stories, seeing what is truth and what is shame attempting to create self- sabotage. At least in typical therapy situations it is possible to take a recurring problem and unwrap it until the origin of belief is discovered. Finding that original thought can lend itself to creating a strategy which more often than not results in a gratifying emotional breakthrough and the ability to face life with a fresh perspective.

Working with such fresh and obvious PTSD forced me to develop a whole new arsenal of strategies, with Esther next to me at the helm. If typical therapy is trying to resolve a problem, mindset, or behavior then adding PTSD to the mix is like covering the initial issue with spikes, disguising it as something else, hiding it, and then precluding it with a panic attack. I'm no stranger to anxiety, both personally and professionally, but anxiety with trauma riding shotgun was a new beast altogether.

So, what do you do when a teenager who has witnessed mass murder, has run through the blood of victims, and who has spent an entire night hiding in a bathroom believing they are alone in a city under siege turns up hyperventilating in your office because the classroom next door showed a movie with gun fire and they heard the all too familiar pop pop pop through the classroom wall, but also they failed a math test and yes they are still fighting with their mom? How do you untangle trauma from typical problems and somehow work to find a peaceful resolution for all of it?

This is the answer everyone wants.

And the only answer that I have is that you do. . .everything. Except for the times when you do nothing.

I've always known that there is no universal mental health strategy that works for everyone. During this time, I also learned that what worked for one child on one day might not work the next, but could work again a few days later. Unless it didn't. So, the best thing that we could do was to come up with as many options as possible to keep the panic at bay and just start ticking through them until heart rates had settled and breathing was normal and we could get to the issue at hand. If there actually was an issue at hand, because trauma and anxiety love to create problems where none genuinely exist. We deep breathed, we went for walks, we pet the dog, we colored endless mandalas, we did grounding exercises, we journaled, and sometimes we just cried it out. We went to the greenhouse to touch the succulents and to the cafeteria to find something sugary. We wrote gratitude lists and rattled off all of reasons why the present moment was a safe one. We sat and did nothing, while I listened quietly. Some days one of those strategies worked. Some days it took several of them. Other days nothing worked no matter what we tried and kids retreated home to the safety of under the covers.

Before you write this off as irrelevant to your own life and page ahead for more of Jill's adorable dog pictures, let's pause to consider a few things. You may not be servicing youth in any capacity and you may not be a mental health worker. I pray it is unlikely that you will ever be victim of a mass shooting or find yourself loving a family member through that particular trauma. However, the odds that you and the ones that you love will escape life without a healthy dose of trauma are sadly very low. Let's all explore childhood trauma together, shall we?

The Adverse Childhood Experience questionnaire is widely studied as a way to gauge childhood trauma. Its partner resiliency questionnaire attempts to predict resiliency later in life. The ACE quiz, as it is known, only asks about ten potentially traumatic childhood incidents, five related to self and five related to family members. Using this scale, someone who perceived growing up in an unloving home, had parents who separated or divorced, reports being spoken down to or humiliated as a child, and had someone in the home who either abused alcohol or was depressed will score high enough to be considered a serious risk for both toxic stress related disease and social/emotional problems in adulthood. The ACE is one of many tools available to gauge the impact of our experiences on our physical and mental health. While all of these tools vary they agree on one thing: stress creates a breeding ground for illness and dysfunction later in life.

This format also considers that there are many factors that can exacerbate these results. Suppose you take the quiz and you are able to check only of one of the ten factors. Great. You can pat yourself on the back and congratulate yourself on surviving childhood relatively unscathed. But wait, what if you checked just one but had exacerbating circumstances? Were you the victim of bullying or racism? Did you lose a caregiver? Were you diagnosed with a serious illness or did you suffer any form of abandonment? Sit back down and buckle up because you, my friend, may just be a survivor of trauma.

I do want to be clear here that I am in no way suggesting that surviving a mass shooting is the same as having your parents get divorced. Those who came through that experience needed dedicated, focused, and continuous support. It would be horribly wrong to minimize anything about that terrifying experience and that is not my intention. Nor do I believe that we all need to put on our victim hats, bemoan the sheer unfairness of childhood, and take a pass for life based on what happened during our formative years. Not at all. I do believe that we all owe it to ourselves to do some soul searching on just what kind of baggage we are carrying around and then dig a little deeper to see how it impacts us on the daily, because the hard truth is that unchecked it most likely will affect us on the daily. Simply put, trauma is trauma.

My school prides itself on loving on our students and creating a family atmosphere. Las Vegas can be a transient community and the teen years can be difficult no matter where they are spent. Those facts coupled with our Christian mission to prepare believers for the afterlife drives us to love our kids as best we can. We strive to know our kids well and be a resource when they struggle with hard times. It is common for our counseling office to get phone calls from hospital rooms or to be a first stop following traumatic news. We have carefully thought out policies and plans for all sorts of different tragedies and emergencies.

Our school community rallied around our 1 October survivors, which was the right thing to do. We worked to discover the best ways to help these girls and how to support them as they navigated the school days and prepared for college. While it was right and good and I am proud to have served on such a caring team of people, it did give me pause. The trauma these girls had survived was well known and the symptoms of PTSD were glaring. It was natural that we would relentlessly move through every strategy we had to help them work through it. I realized that I needed to be as relentless in dealing with kids and adults who were suffering less obvious effects of more hidden trauma. The very public ACE study results casually points out that childhood trauma is common and there is a direct link between it and the development of issues as we grow. Big issues like chronic illness, depression, suicide risk, and being the perpetrator or victim of violent crime. If a score of four more on the ACE can be so casually attained and that score means a predisposition to issues down the road, then how are we not learning strategies to heal and cope and grow at every turn?

Let's go back to doing everything, except when you do nothing.

As adults, we need a full toolbox of coping skills so that we can teach the little people in our lives how to cope. This isn't the same as self-care, the oft wielded shield of therapists. Think of self-care as the gas that you put in your tank so that you can keep driving. This trauma toolbox is where you keep the tools that will extinguish the lit match headed for that gas tank. I want to take a moment a very passionately admit that there are far more experty-experts out there than me. If this chapter strikes a chord, start googling and start researching. Better yet, book an appointment with a counselor and start exploring the knots in your head. From my humble corner of the world, this is the best in strategy that I have to offer. Again, I wish it was a neat checklist that was universal for everyone. Take what helps, toss the rest.

Severely traumatized or not, we all know the feeling. That feeling where you realize you are seconds away from reacting entirely irrationally or are actually in the midst of reacting irrationally. I liken it to my first solid month post-partum after each baby, the out of body feeling of watching a crazy person try to do life while crying. The bonus kicker on this is that you get to wallow in days of social anxiety about how you reacted and how it could be perceived. Sometimes this feeling isn't so poignant, rather it creeps in as malaise, self-loathing, or self-doubt. It is the voice that slides around in our heads reminding us that we aren't good enough, we aren't smart enough, and at the end of the day no one really likes us anyway. All of the self-care in the world can't ward off this kind of shame spiral. Whether you are on day one of acting like a psychopath or day ten of chest crushing self-doubt, we usually wind up zeroing in on one toxic thought and allowing it to work itself into full blown anxiety and total derailment.

I very recently took a hard turn down this road myself when I woke up in a crushing anxiety attack. I was tired and knew I had a long day ahead of me and my thoughts quickly shame spiraled into anger and resentment that I work such long hours, have so many demands placed on me, deal with the constant stream of texts and emails with questions and requests for support, and also juggle my own family's needs.

You know, the things that come along with all of those answered prayers for an amazing career, the hard work put in to build it, and the blessing of a family? Cue the tiny violins. Clearly (eye roll) no one has ever had it worse than me.

I kicked the morning off by starting a fight with my husband about how unfair it is that every other mother on the planet got to stay home or work part time for at least a portion of their kids' lives. By the way, now is not the time to point out that this isn't even true or that my kids are old enough to be basically self-sufficient. Anyway, everyone knows that an idle Wednesday morning at 6 am is the perfect time to blindside your spouse with a rant about why I didn't get to stay at home with the now fifteen year old baby.

Shockingly, that didn't make me feel better although it did pretty much ruin Zack's morning. Anxiety does love to be shared and passed around.

Esther, the kids, and I loaded into the car to head to school. I'm embarrassed to say that the kids picked up on all of this nonsense and started offering back to me the kind of words I give to them when they tantrum about the unfairness of our comfortable life in our stable loving family.

"Mom. If you didn't do what you did we wouldn't even have Esther. We wouldn't get to go to Faith. We love it at Faith. You wouldn't have all of your friends there. You wouldn't get to help kids. I'm sorry you're tired."

My daughter even sent me a sweet text later in the morning thanking me for working so hard for her.

It didn't help.

So, while trudging through my day, which turned out to involved a revolving door of crying students and demanding parents, I also tried the following things to make myself feel better:

- I ranted at friends over text about the unfairness of my life. (Again, so embarrassing. Thank God I have patient friends.)

- I online purchased an expensive pair of shoes and a few shirts I've had my eye on.

- I ordered food delivery and wolfed down a steaming bowl of veggie pho, without really tasting it, while returning calls on speaker phone. I also consumed an alarming number of Hershey's kisses, without tasting those either.

- I dragged Esther on a three mile run after school, not to relax but to punish myself for all of the chocolate. No exercise endorphins here. Just one angry little Doodle who thought she would get to play some fetch and maybe do some swimming.

- I hauled Evan to the store after his practice was over to buy wine and more chocolate and snacks. All of which I consumed while trolling around social media where I made myself sick with jealousy at all of the people I convinced myself had it "easier." Ironic, considering that I myself am guilty of posting adorable puppy pictures to hide an evening of animal urine and feces and a dance competition fraught with tension. You'd think I would have learned by now that social media is a liar.

- Full of wine, chocolate, and inexplicably hot Cheetos (Yes. Yes, I am a 40something adult woman with reasonable knowledge of nutrition.) I rounded out my evening with a too hot Epsom salt bath. Laying in the nearly boiling scented water I contemplated how disgusted I was with myself and also how stressed I was about the next day. At that point I was over twelve hours into some steady wallowing.

If I had been able to take my own advice and behave like an actual adult, let alone someone trained in mental health, I would have stopped that train in its tracks. What is it about people and our refusal to do what we know will help? I don't know about you, but I sometimes feel like I have a deep seated masochistic streak when it comes to sinking into these kinds of spirals. It's like the emotional equivalent of ripping a scab off for no good reason.

Had I decided to leave the scab picking alone I would have woken up and started the day with a prayer journal and not a rant. I would have done some yoga and practiced a little deep breathing. Instead of blindsiding my husband I would have sat long enough to let the emotions raging through me tell me what their names actually were. Maybe I even would have journaled them out a bit.

Anger? No. Outside of being actively wronged by another human being, rarely is anger actually anger. It is usually fear or insecurity or disappointment trying to masquerade about like a tougher and less vulnerable emotion. I wasn't truly angry about my job and I wasn't lobbying to quit and stay home because Zack had let me down by failing to provide that option. I was actually cycling through fear and vastly doubting myself. My own baggage tells me how could someone like me be able to do a job like this one? How could someone from such a broken home possibly be a good mother? It was way easier to divert that emotion into the idea that I was just a victim set up for failure as a professional and as a parent and then rage about all of the injustices that led to this sorry state.

What a different day it would have been if I had first brought it God and accepted peace from Him. If I needed more I could have approached my family with my doubts instead of my anger. They would have loved me, reassured me, and sent me into the world confident enough to face what lay head. I would have extinguished the match before it blew up my gas tank and led me to a day of terrible choices trying to refill it.

I hate the word trigger. It hits me in the gut as a word that causes guards to fly up on all sides, reminding me of the meme of the weeping college student at a football game who will sadly forever symbolize a total lack of resilience. Please forgive me as I forgive myself for using the word I hate most, second only to the word supper, but we have to learn to stop these emotional storms and decipher what the real emotion is, where its origin lies, and if there is any truth to it. This practice is incredibly more difficult when PTSD is involved, as there are so many more layers to unravel. Those of us with a standard amount of baggage can learn to do this fairly easily with some practice. In turn, it's been incredibly helpful while working with students who are struggling to emotionally regulate.

Once you've deep breathed, petted a dog, colored a book, screamed into a pillow, or walked it off to where your fight or flight response is under control and you have some measure of calm, I recommend the following series of questions to work back to the actual cause of your emotional storm.

1. What are the emotions I am currently feeling? List all of them, even the tiny ones bubbling under the surface.

   (In my example, I would have listed anger, exhaustion, resentment.)

2. Is there a theme to the emotions? If not, which one do I feel the most?

   (There overlying feeling is being stressed about the day ahead.)

3. Is it possible to summarize the problem these feelings are surrounding? Statements that being with "I feel" are super handy here.

   (I feel like there is too much being asked of me between school and home.)

4. Is this problem true? Does it exactly exist? If it does, stop and start creating an action plan. If it is not a real problem but a lie being told in my head, what is the truth it is masking?

   (This is not true. No unfair demands are placed on me at work or at home. It's not that I shouldn't have to handle my responsibilities, it's that I am afraid that I can't.)

5. What emotions are driving the actual truth?

   (Fear. Insecurity. Self-doubt.)

6. How do I get a handle on these emotions?

   (Junk food, wine, and self-flagellation for the win! Just kidding.)

These secret underlying emotions need to be written down, prayed about, and spoken out loud to a loved one. They need to be actively countered with examples of why they aren't true. We need to own those voices that whisper from the suitcase of our past, do a little digging, and move forward in the truth to truly face the challenge in front of us.

Chapter 20

Is Your Circle Helping or Hurting You?

WHEN WE LEFT OFF with Queen Esther she had just wrapped up hosting her first banquet for her King and for Haman. She was calm and steady, did not blurt out all of her secrets and accusations, and demurely invited the King and Haman back for a second banquet the next night. She also plied Xerxes with enough wine and food that he woke up with the wine and meat sweats requesting that the royal records be read. Haman, for his part, attended the first banquet and went whistling home in high spirits about the invitation to a second banquet alone with such important people.

Like many scheming social climbing men, Haman had an equally ambitious wife waiting for him at home. I once saw a bumper sticker slapped on a minivan that stopped me in my tracks. It boasted the symbol of a branch of our military and proclaimed "You will address me by my husband's rank."

What?

I have some concerns. I mean, I don't want to take away from the stress of being a military wife. I've had a small taste of it as a law enforcement wife and I realize the challenges are unique and can be overwhelming. I have not had to endure countless moves and reassignments or the reality of having my spouse deployed. That said, just how hard was boot camp, deployment, learning to excel well enough to rise through the ranks, and putting in the endless hours of grinding work for this woman?

Oh wait. That was her husband that did those things?

It also makes me sad to see women taking their identity from the careers of their spouses. I am all for love, support, and being incredibly proud of them. I believe that teamwork makes the dream work. But there is also so much to be said for the reward that comes with building your own life and accomplishments. I would prefer to be proud of my husband's rank, but be addressed by my own.

Anyway, Haman's wife Zeresh was most certainly driving around the citadel of Susa with a bumper sticker slapped on her horse's rump instructing the commoners to address her by her husband's rank. She was probably the kind of woman who was secretly cheered when Vashti was deposed, competitive and excited to revel in the downfall of a beautiful and powerful woman. Maybe she even sported a very distinctive haircut and demanded to speak to the manager when shopping in the market stalls in Susa. We are introduced to Zeresh the morning of Esther's first banquet. This particular morning Haman rushes home from work, pausing only to pass Mordecai in the courtyard and be extra furious that his nemesis is still not respecting him nor showing outward fear of him. He rages internally for a bit and then collects himself, bursting into his home to gloat to his wife that he had been invited to a second royal banquet with just the King and Queen. This is a big honor, even for the King's right hand man.

Zeresh is delighted. She's been training her whole life to be married to the second most important man in all of the land and has always encouraged Haman to stop at nothing to achieve this goal. For his part, Haman has some more good vibes to get off of his chest so he gathers a few friends and commits to full on swaggering about his position and influence, his children and his wealth, his ability to command the king's ear, and how he was the only one invited to the king's banquet to dine with the royal couple. Zeresh basks in his accomplishments and his buddies are appropriately impressed. Suddenly, Haman is crestfallen. None of this will mean anything, he laments out loud, so long as that Jew Mordecai is still on the King's payroll.

Oh, for crying out loud. Is it typically human or horribly narcissistic to be in the midst of being admired for accomplishments only to be side tracked by a petty vendetta? To have so much bitterness built up and unresolved that it spoils every moment of happiness and contentment? Or to succumb to the thinking that we still just need one more thing in order to be satisfied? I can't decide if I identify with Haman in this moment or if I'm repulsed by him. Probably some of both. Not one to let her husband risk losing the chance to get ahead, Zeresh is quick to offer a solution. A very grisly solution.

Build gallows. Make them 75 feet high. When you get back to the royal palace ask Xerxes to have Mordecai hanged on it. He's already agreed to your plan to eradicate the Jews, so it should be no big deal. Then, you go on and enjoy yourself a nice meal with the King. You've earned it!

75 feet, which seems like an arbitrary number, is actually pretty significant. The city walls of Susa were most likely 75 feet high. The prominent buildings in town were probably about the same height. This paradigm of grace and beauty was actually suggesting that the gallows be built high enough that all of the people in the land could witness Mordecai's death and so that there was a very obvious warning to anyone who thought about disrespecting her husband. Haman found this suggestion absolutely delightful and was probably congratulating himself on choosing such a brilliant mate. Even more disturbing, the friends he had gathered were all eagerly nodding in agreement to this plan.

Clearly, community is important. Obviously we need the friends who drag us through hard times, sit silently with us when we are in robe tearing mourning, and who celebrate our achievements as their own. But Haman's crew? This is a lesson in watching and knowing your inner circle. Friends should not blindly agree with you, be so shallow that they do not care enough to speak up when you are on a path to destruction, or enable your terrible choices. Haman's friends are the ones who pour you too many drinks and then agree that you are fine to drive home. They are the ones that justify your bad choices and encourage you to hang on to feelings of bitterness and to seek revenge for petty grudges. The type that find themselves nodding in agreement about a 75 foot gallows built for no reason other than because a buddy felt slighted.

What's truly sad about this whole thing is that the wheels that had been set in motion still had time to be stopped. If Haman's friends had paused and thought it through or if they had loved him enough to speak the truth in love, the outcome of this book could have been quite different. If Zeresh was not so blinded by her ambition she could have soothed her husband's ego, assuring him that he was important and valued and that he did not need to be threatened by some man in a lower rank who happened to have different religious beliefs. If any number of these people had enough integrity to speak, perhaps Haman would have been swayed. There was still time.

Haman could have returned to work the next day emboldened by his wife's love and the wise and peaceful counsel of his friends. Granted, he would still have faced a day of parading Mordecai around on horseback like a common town crier, but let's imagine for a moment that he survived that with ego intact. Maybe, and this could be too farfetched, he could have come into work so secure with himself that he was able to make some small talk with Mordecai as they spent the day together and discovered some common ground. Maybe even some things that he liked about the guy. They could have chatted, split some almonds and pomegranates for lunch, and gone back to the royal palace as civil coworkers. Haman could have talked to the King prior to the banquet and called the whole thing off. He could have even humbly admitted that his ego had gotten ahold of him. After all, the King was no stranger to rash decisions led by ego.

If Haman had been secure enough to do all this, the outcome would have been different, not just for himself but for so many others. His initial beef with Mordecai was one of long standing ancestral differences. What a salve to political wounds it would have been if the two men could have presented the appearance of tolerance, if not actual friendship. What a fantastic victory for the Jews in the court of public opinion to have a high ranking official make peace with them. The Jewish people had been living in fear for days that not only did Haman want them all dead, but that the King wholeheartedly supported it. It must have been terrifying. I have to imagine that even after Haman died and Esther was revealed as Jewish, there must have been some fear and mistrust of Xerxes that lingered. If Haman had been able to halt his own plot, it most likely would have put a lot of minds at ease.

If only Haman had a wife with some discernment and the ability to create a soft place for him to land. If only she hadn't been blinded by her own consuming need for reflective importance she may have been able to counsel him wisely. Likewise, his friends missed a big opportunity to potentially to right a ship headed for disaster.

Take a look at your circle. Can you speak the truth in love to the ones closest to you? There is power and grace in loving someone enough to risk being uncomfortable for the sake of saving them.

Even more uncomfortable, is your circle brave enough to check you back? We all need cheerleaders, the people who endlessly root for us and genuinely celebrate our big wins. However, if your biggest cheerleaders are only affirming you and not pushing you to grow and confront bad behavior it is likely time for some hard honest conversations.

Chapter 21

You Can Take the Dog Out of Vegas

MY SCHOOL IS VERY big on mission work. We believe that to whom much is given, much is demanded and we do our very best to train our students up with servant's hearts. This thinking begins in the middle school with our November all school service day, which is one of my most favorite days of the year. We dispatch close to a thousand middle schoolers and adults out into the Las Vegas community to serve in as many ways as possible. Students help in elementary schools, read to seniors, pack lunches, sort clothing donations, and deep clean food pantries. They do crafts with veterans and serve lunches to the homeless. I love watching the kids come streaming back onto campus, eager to both talk about their experiences and to learn how to volunteer more. Even better, the kids travel to serve in their advisory class, which is like our homeroom, and the advisories stay in touch with the organization they serve throughout the school year often organizing drives for supplies or exchanging letters with seniors in assisted living homes.

It gives me all of the warm and fuzzies. There is no greater gift than the opportunity to serve your community. Having a bad day? Give back somehow. It works every time.

The opportunities to serve grow along with the students. Our missions director, Julie, works tirelessly to foster opportunities. Kids have the chance to travel to Mexico to volunteer with an organization that builds houses and to Alaska to work with variety of community resources. We've sent kids all over the country to work in different ways, but the one thing all of the trips have in common is that the kids come back changed. There is just something about the chance to make someone else's life better that is both humbling and empowering.

Esther's amazing photographer, Jill, is married to another teacher at our school. Jill and T.J. lead a mission trip to L.A. every spring where they have built connections with a homeless shelter and a children's after school program in a disadvantaged neighborhood. During Esther's first puppy year terrorizing my office Jill would often mention how great it would be to take Esther along on that trip.

'She's such a sweet soul. She would open so many doors with people." Jill would remark as baby Esther picked up the pillows from my couch and violently shook them.

"I can just imagine the people at the shelter and the kids from the neighborhood just melting if they met Esther. She is so calming." Jill would sigh wistfully as baby Esther darted away from me to investigate the magical tater tot bush and I dragged her back by her orange teddy bear feet.

In the fall of Esther's first full year of working Jill and T.J. casually asked me if I would help chaperone that trip. I tend to blindly agree to anything that is asked of me if it is further than four months away and I often forget to mark it on my calendar. This creates problems for me, as I am double booked more often than not. I guess I live my life assuming that Jesus is going to come back before I'm actually faced with a deadline or commitment. Knowing my dirty secret of constant haphazard over commitment, Jill wisely forced me to add it to my calendar while she was still in my office. As she was leaving she quickly muttered under her breath that Esther was committed to come along as well. Then she scurried out.

I wasn't too worried. Obviously Jesus would come back before I had to pack this dog into a van and take her out on the mission field. It would be fine.

A few months later Jesus still had not come back and Jill and T.J. were texting to ask if I was good to drive one of the vans to California and if Esther had any special requests. I laughed at the story of my life, I get assignments and Esther gets special treatment, but still didn't really believe that the actual day of the trip would roll around. Until suddenly we were gathered in the front parking lot of the school loading luggage and Esther's travel kennel into one of the school's SUVs. Esther had no idea what was coming, but was delighted to find herself included in something out of the ordinary.

We were taking a larger group of kids than they had ever taken on this particular trip. It was also an oddly diverse group, spread across grades and social circles. Typically, kids will sign up with a few friends for these trips and then over the course of the experience the micro social groups will merge into a cohesive group. I didn't realize until we were getting ready to leave just how unique of a crew we had assembled, pairs of friends or single students who didn't know the others well. Ever the expert, T.J. had hosted a series of icebreaker meetings and devotions in the weeks leading up to the trip, but the air of awkwardness still hung.

I shoved the last of Esther's treats, toys, bowls, blankies, assorted leashes, vests, shoes, and bandanas into the back of the vehicle, along with the small backpack of my stuff. I didn't know the students riding with me very well, but they were all excited to be with Esther. I tried to ignore my growing anxiety about all of the things that could go wrong, checked the sky one more time for any sign of the Second Coming, and climbed into the driver's seat. The drive to California flew by as the atmosphere in the car quickly thawed. The kids reveled in the novelty of heading out on a school day with the Comfort Dog. Esther, safely belted in, soaked up all of the love and excitement. Her nose quivered as she watched the highway fly by and tried to signal to the boy next to her that her treats were right behind him.

My anxiety spiked again as we pulled into the motel. I knew we were serving in a rough area and I am not a princess when it comes to accommodations, no matter what anyone says. I've done my share of time in sketchy neighborhoods and once was even trapped in what could only be described as a murder motel when a spring snowstorm left Dan and I stranded with a group of kids in Indianapolis. I know how to check for bed bugs and when to wear flip flops in the shower. I am good to request towels from a clerk hiding behind a bullet proof partition. It's fine.

What I wasn't prepared for was a motel with a high fenced in parking lot, a tiny patch of weeds that promised to hide a good deal of broken glass, and no sidewalks in sight. Not only did Esther and I walk or run a few miles every day, but I had no idea where I was going to take her to go to the bathroom. She refuses to go on cement, she's too fancy for that, but there was no dirt, turf, or safe grass to be seen. I also considered that I would need to take her out by myself at night. I pictured Esther and I, alone in the dark, navigating the broken glass with the light from my iPhone while I pled with her to go potty and prayed no one surprised me in the darkness.

It's fine. Jesus will probably come back before she needs to go to the bathroom, right?

I took her on an initial lap around the motel parking lot while everyone else checked in and discovered that one lap was roughly .15 of a mile. So, at just fourteen laps we would be close to our normal walking distance. I loaded up a few podcasts to prepare for our inevitable laps and started hauling all of Esther's supplies up the two flights of stairs to our hotel room, thankful that my years of being a dance mom Sherpa had prepared me for this.

Mai, our super adorable admissions director, drew the short stick and was sharing the room with us. She dodged the orange missile as Esther launched herself from bed to bed pausing only to sniff in a corner that may or may not have been a crime scene at one point. Eventually I snagged her midflight and snapped her leash on so that we could head downstairs to poolside where Jill and T.J. had gathered the kids for pizza and devotions. The kids, scattered around the pool, cheered at Esther's approach and everyone gave her a pat as she trotted by. Faced with the pool, I could see that Esther had some hard decisions to make.

"NO SWIMMING." She stared up at me as if trying to gauge how serious I was, then dramatically flopped down next to a group of girls. She behaved for all of the meeting, taking her time moving from student to student and accepting the snuggles while trying to discreetly see if anyone had any pizza left.

Following devotions I set out into the dark parking lot to try to convince her to potty which went surprisingly well, despite the audience of teenagers watching as they headed up to their rooms. Shameless, this one is. The two of us made our way up to our room, where Mai and I discovered that rooming with a dog who is enjoying her first night in a motel is a lot like rooming with a toddler who has never been away from home before. Delighted, punch drunk, and refusing to settle down, Esther grinned ear from ear as she hopped around the room and rolled on the beds.

We eventually got her tucked in her kennel where she snored through the night, exhausted by a day of adventure. The next morning, we met for breakfast in the hotel's lobby and were greeted with some bad news from our trip leaders. The plan was to work at three sites with three different organizations. The homeless shelter had called to report it had been the scene of a fatal stabbing the night before and would not be accepting any volunteers. Then the leader of the second organization phoned to say that he had a sudden death in the family and would not be available to work with us. This left only the after school program for disadvantaged children, which is a tremendous program but could not accommodate the amount of kids that we had with us all at once. The original plan was to cycle the kids in three groups through the three sites over the course of the trip. Months of meticulous planning and communication by our trip leaders had disintegrated in the course of an hour with just two phone calls. We chaperones stared at each other while the kids milled around eating bagels and Esther slept under our table. Then we got busy making phone calls.

We found a small Lutheran elementary school in the infancy of its existence not too far away that was happy to have workers to clean, organize supplies, and play with the kids. A local church was excited to have help packing Vacation Bible School boxes to send overseas. That church had a relationship with the nursing home across the street and they would love a visit from some kids and a dog. We hastily sketched out a new itinerary, trying to consider the craziness of Los Angeles traffic and the hours and limitations of the organizations we were working with. Then we did what you do when you are out serving a cause bigger than yourself; we gave it God.

My first stop with Esther was at the after school program. It was in a gang afflicted neighborhood and this community center aimed to catch kids at a young age, keep them of the streets after school, and hopefully steer them toward safe choices. There was tutoring available along with a steady stream of snacks and activities.

It so happens that Esther and I both love snacks and activities.

We arrived before the young ones and took a quick tour with one of beautiful souls in charge. She warned me that the kids would probably be pretty apprehensive about Esther at first. This wasn't a neighborhood where dogs were kept for snuggle buddies. Dogs were for protection and were not to be approached or messed with. Having a dog around that you could just pet would most likely be an experience the kids needed to warm up to. As the children streamed in a little while later it was quickly obvious that her predictions were correct. They all stopped short when they saw Esther laying in the main room and then took a wide berth around her to avoid getting too close. I kept her in her down stay while the teenagers that were with me tried to convince the littles that she was safe. I rolled her onto her back while the one of my more patient students tried to lure a little girl in to give Esther a quick rub on her belly.

"She's so soft. See? And she doesn't move at all. You don't have to be scared. Just try it once." Soon tiny fingers were disappearing in the fuzz along Esther's tummy. The little girl squealed with delight while Esther heaved a contended sigh that caused her mouth to fall a little open. Our new small friend stopped petting.

"Those are her teeth?" She gestured at the little round teeth visible between Esther's shiny black lips.

"Yep. But she doesn't bite. You don't have to worry." I hoped that the sight of teeth wasn't upsetting and that we weren't undoing the comfort we had gained. The little girl continued to pause.

"I want to touch her teeth." She already had one small finger outstretched toward Esther's mouth but paused to wait for my answer.

"Well. O.k." I wasn't sure what the right answer was, but didn't want to squash her chance to be brave in a safe space. She gently ran her finger down one of Esther's teeth while Esther, still on her back, stared at me out of the corner of her eye as if to ask if this was allowed. Eventually more kids came over to meet Esther Bean and I was proud of both students and dog as I watched my kids talk about her with the younger ones.

That pride would continue all weekend. At the small Lutheran school, we toured classrooms where Esther was met with squeals and giggles. My big kids played on the playground with the young ones, comically losing over and over again in a pick-up basketball game, while Esther laid in the grass and accepted pets from all who came over. A teacher's aide brought out a nonverbal Autistic student, who passed an enjoyable 15 minutes in the sun just squeezing Esther's fur gently between his fingers. At the nursing home my students listened patiently as the elderly residents told them about the pets they had owned in their younger days while stroking Esther on the head. One lady burst into tears about missing her dog since being moved into the home and Esther responded by burying her face in the lady's wheel-chair bound legs as my kids scrambled to try to offer her more comfort.

It was also incredibly gratifying to watch the kids connect to each other over the course of the short trip. We had worried that the group was too big, their interests too varied to become fully cohesive. When we had to abandon the original plans and punt we worried that our adult stress would spill over and make the original awkwardness turn into tension. Thankfully, that didn't happen and the group came together quickly. Mai mused to me on the last night of the trip, as Esther jumped up and down on her bed, that the dog had a lot to do with that. There was always a common ground. They could break an awkward silence with someone they didn't know very well with a story about what Esther did that day or how ridiculous it was to watch me endlessly circle the parking lot with her.

Even our laps around the parking lot had the chance to become meaningful. On more than one excursion I had a student ask to join me under the guise of wanting to hang out with Esther. As we walked and walked I would listen to stories of losing a family member, struggling with school, trouble at home, or total confusion about what to do about college.

This trip confirmed that a dog can be the greatest equalizer and the world's best conversation starter. Nothing draws people together and breaks the ice like a dog. Over the last few years I have had people interested in training personal dogs to become therapy dogs visiting nursing homes or after school programs reach out to me. The concerns they voice are usually less about dog training or school programs and more often fears centered around not being trained as a counselor as they venture in to visit facilities. After this trip I can confidently tell them that you don't need to be a counselor to take a dog out to visit people and change the world. I actually discovered that all you need to say in these situations is one statement and one question.

"I can tell that the dog really likes you!" This won't be a lie. The dogs genuinely like everyone. We don't deserve dogs.

"Do you have a dog at home?" The person you are talking to may not have a dog at home, but they will still tell you about a dog they had growing up, a dog a relative had, or a dog they used to drive by. Everyone has a dog story.

That's all it takes to make everyone comfortable and get the conversation started. Dogs truly bring people together.

Chapter 22

Wrapping Things Up in Susa

AT LAST WE'VE COME to the end of the book of Esther. Our queen is busy preparing for her second night hosting Xerxes and Haman at a special banquet. The gallows, freshly shined and 75 feet high as requested, loom large over the city. The king is most likely pregaming somewhere in the palace with some wine or sleeping off the effects of the alcohol he consumed at lunch before getting ready for dinner. Humble Mordecai, still worried about the fate of his people, probably can't help but be a little cheered by his big day of recognition. Haman, humiliated from a day of parading Mordecai around and reminding everyone in the city that his nemesis is a hero who thwarted a murder plot, heads home to prepare for the banquet. He complains bitterly to Zeresh and his friends about what his day entailed, glossing over his murderous plans and focusing on his wounded ego, as he gets ready to head back to the palace for dinner. Hearing that her husband's Jewish foe is currently being held in high esteem panics Zeresh and she pleads with him to pause his evil plot.

To be clear, nothing indicates that Zeresh had a change of heart about wiping out an entire people in order for her husband to get ahead. Instead, she recognizes he is in a battle that he most likely can't currently win. Right hand man or not, suggesting the hanging of the person who recently saved the king's life is not a good look for anyone. It's too little, too late. As she blurts out that he needs to turn this bus around, the eunuchs arrive to whisk Haman away to the banquet.

I know the feeling of sending your spouse out into danger. As much as I find Zeresh distasteful, I pity the amount of hand ringing and regret that night must have held for her as she waited for her husband's return home. The author of Esther carefully points out that the gallows had been constructed specifically to be visible from the Haman family home, probably so that he and Zeresh could gloat together with friends as they watched Mordecai and his people hanging. I'm sure she was able to watch the night's events unfold from her home.

Haman is marched into the banquet by the ever present eunuchs to join the royal couple for happy hour before dinner. Over this glass of wine Xerxes again asks Esther what it is her heart desires. Esther screws up all of her courage, takes a deep breath, and asks the king to please spare her and her people from the slaughter and annihilation that has been planned for them.

The king wonders who planned this, forgetting that he had actually approved the plan not too long ago himself. Esther whispers that it was Haman, throwing Xerxes into a rage so huge that he dismisses himself to the royal garden to take a few deep and sobering breathes. Haman, sensing what lies ahead for him, decides to plead with the softest heart in the room and sidles up to Esther on her couch. Oh Haman. If Xerxes is the king of Persia, Haman is the crown prince of bad timing. The king stomps back into the room at precisely that moment and believes that Haman is attempting to molest Esther.

Without this, Haman may have had a chance at cooling his heels in the prison dungeon for a bit and hopefully pleading his case later. It was all a misunderstanding, I love the Jews, remember who just spent the day parading his best friend Mordecai around? He most certainly would have been demoted but he possibly could have had his life spared. Instead, he enraged the guy who didn't think twice about banishing his first wife for refusing to appear before him by giving the appearance of attempting to make unwanted advances on the new young queen.

As the king stands consumed with his rage one of his eunuchs, possibly one who had been rooting for Esther since her early days, helpfully pointed out that there were some fresh new gallows that had just been built over by Haman's house. Maybe those would work? This revelation sealed Haman's fate and he was hanging from them within the hour. All of his greed, ego, plotting, and scheming had finally caught up with him.

With Haman's body still swinging from the gallows, Xerxes awarded Esther his entire estate, which she appointed Mordecai to oversee. The king had retrieved his signet ring from Haman's lifeless hand and presented it to Mordecai as well, elevating him to the highest position in the kingdom. And then, there was most likely a very awkward and tense pause between the cousins and the king, because there was still the very problematic matter of the edict to murder all of the Jews. As we saw with the decree to banish Vashti, the king could not take back an edict once it had been announced. Esther, Mordecai, and the Jewish people had not yet arrived at safety, even after the hanging of Haman. Finally, Esther fell at the king's feet weeping and begging for him to halt the plan. He ordered her to rise while he considered how he would do this.

Probably already used to having to solve problems on behalf of her husband, Esther quickly pointed out that while he couldn't take the edict back he could absolutely just issue a new one. A better one. One that would not just keep from harming the Jewish people, but would actually help them. The royal secretaries were assembled and a new edict was composed with the help of Mordecai. As it often is with these kinds of terrible times, silver linings quickly emerged for the Jews after years of fear and injustice. God has a knack for using awful circumstance to not only teach lessons but offer great gains. The Jews had been enslaved in Susa for generations and while they had recently gained some rights they were still far from being recognized as equal among the Persians. The reveal of the plot of Haman and the realization of how easily and quickly the Jews had almost been eradicated sparked some justice in the city through the king's new edict. The Jews were awarded the right to assemble and the right to protect themselves. They could finally fight back against any entity threatening to do them harm. In every province of the king this edict was met with feasting and celebrations.

Mordecai, after years of aggression from Haman and his cronies, left the king's courts that day in blue and white royal robes. I have to believe that he had questioned his place in the royal court over the years of mistreatment, probably occasionally succumbing to fear and self pity. He took in his orphaned niece, risked his own life to save his people, and did his job faithfully and intelligently. Mordecai is an example to us of so many character traits. Perhaps most of all he is a lesson in the reward of remaining calm and steady, working hard and staying the course all while trusting in God's plan.

Things are not quite over in this chapter of Susa's history, though. The Jews, with their new right to assemble and to protect themselves, are quick to realize that Haman had a whole large crowd of people who not only wholeheartedly supported his murder plot and hated the Jews but who are also still a danger to the Jewish people. They are not only still hateful and blood thirsty, they are also likely holding the Jewish people responsible for the death of their leader. Eventually the Jews had no choice but to assemble under Mordecai's leadership to overtake their enemies. In the citadel of Susa five hundred enemies of the Jews were put to the sword. Throughout the provinces of Xerxes over seventy-five thousand were killed. Of this great number were the ten grown sons of Haman. They were not only put to death, but hung from the gallows where Haman met his fate.

The phrase "sins of the father" is often bandied about and debated. It seems really unfair that a child would be held accountable for something that happened generations back, and it would be. What this phrase actually refers to is that the damage we cause as parents will certainly affect the generations to come. A drunken dad is likely to raise a child who will eventually struggle with addiction or mental health issues if the cycle is not broken. Statistics clearly tell us that children raised with violence in the home are far more likely to commit or accept abuse in adulthood. Racism, prejudice, and misogyny will be passed done like family heirlooms until a generation is able to break free from that sinful thinking. While it is entirely possible that Haman's sons were innocent, blameless, and hung solely to eradicate his sinful family lineage, I have to think that the sins of prejudice and hatred had been firmly passed down to them not only by Haman but by the embittered Zeresh. They were likely dangerous in their own right, plotting against the Jews, motivated by revenge, and pursing the agenda once pushed by their father.

From all of the lessons we take from Haman about how not to live, this is the final one. What are you modeling and passing on to the young people in your life? What is the legacy you will leave?

Chapter 23

With a Little Bit of Gratitude

MORDECAI QUICKLY BUILT A name for himself as a wise and powerful leader. With all of the good things happening for the Jewish people, he was enlightened enough to know that human memory for good times can be very short lived. We quickly forget the mountaintops when we are back in the valleys of life. Mordecai had all of the events in the book of Esther recorded to serve as a reminder of God's deliverance and grace to His people. He encouraged the Jewish holiday of Purim to be observed, a joyful holiday of feasting and gift giving. Esther, on her own authority, confirmed that Purim should indeed be celebrated as a time that the Jews found relief from their enemies, had sorrow turn to joy, and had mourning become celebration. Purim remains an important and happy holiday for the Jewish people today.

These are the last of the lessons we can gather from this book. Write down the good times, so that you can remember them when things get hard again. If you don't actively look for those good moments, there is a chance you will miss them altogether. There are times of great joy and deep despair just ahead of all of us. The royal cousins of Susa wisely remind us that we need to be looking for the good time and writing them down daily.

I use this as a counseling strategy with kids who are struggling with low level anxiety or depressive thoughts. Every night before bed, write down five good things from the day. Actually write it down, don't just lay in bed and think it hard. If you can't think of five things, then it's time to write ten and get really basic. Lying in bed? Great. Let's be thankful for the bed. Turned on the water to brush your teeth? Let's be thankful for running water. By the way, kiddo, I am going to ask you to show me your gratitude lists at least once a week so you'd better be doing them.

I'm usually met with a fair amount of eye rolling and sighing, but after twenty plus years in education and two kids of my own I am immune to that sort of thing. They are disbelieving, but they comply not only because we have the best kids at our school but also because no one likes feeling awful and will generally try just about anything to start feeling better. This super simple trick works, even if it can take a while. I don't read the kids' lists, I let them share what they want, but it is always cool to hear the lists evolve from begrudging gratitude for a pillow to genuine recognition and thankfulness for the kindness of another person.

The accountability piece is a huge part of it. As humans we are desperate for a pass from responsibility. A gratitude list is just one more thing to check off of the to do list and it is easy to pass it up. It's not so easy to forget it when you have the responsibility of texting it to a group chat every morning. It's a habit my dance mom posse and I adopted a few years back and one that has become such an important part of the morning. On the days that I don't feel like being grateful, I see the lists of five good things start coming in from the other three and it is the very best kind of peer pressure. I wish I could tell you that I am so incredibly enlightened that my lists are thorough and well thought out, carefully scribed accounts of the extraordinary moments in life that I am blessed with.

They are not.

They most often look like this list that I sent out the other morning:

1. Coffee

2. Esther getting a bath

3. A run with Amber

4. Seeing Karen and Paul Pullmann last night

5. Zack being home last night

It's not earth shattering stuff, but it is a great way to start the morning. It's actually backed by a fair amount of science. When we know we have to report good things, we start actively looking for good things to report. Over time, this active seeking of positive things trains the brain to start looking for the good rather than fixating on the not so good. While this great thinking won't always save us from the spiral that comes with negative thoughts, it does indeed help us both resist it and bounce back from it faster. Any time we can interrupt negative thinking, it needs to be counted as a victory.

Like so many people, my anxiety takes me to my knees at times. I need to remember to pray every time I'm down there, but it's always tempting to wallow. I've always struggled with connecting thoughts that aren't connected. For example, I'll be driving along on the highway and I will miss my exit despite the map's constant warnings that it is approaching. Chagrined by my inability to tell directions or gauge exactly how far away four hundred feet really is, I'll think "I'm a terrible mother."

The examples are endless. Forgetting to return a phone call means that I cannot be trusted. Cooking junk food from the freezer to survive a last minute family dinner means that I didn't take undergrad seriously enough and I should be embarrassed about how poorly I did in some of my classes. Maybe it's time to figure out my actual graduating GPA and force myself to shame hole for a while about it just to get it all out of my system. Problems loom as giant issues, needing to be faced and generally having possible resolution. Anxiety lurks in corners whispering that something terrible is coming but it isn't going to ruin the surprise. Shame hops onto anxiety's back to let you know that you brought all of this onto yourself. It shouldn't be a shock that we need to fill our heads with as many moments of gratitude and joy as possible to combat all of the sadness, stress, and sin that can lurk in there.

This book actually came from trying to do that. I would wake up early every day and try to just offload the emotions and thoughts in my head. As Esther came home and grew up I realized that for all of the stress and potential embarrassment, she just brought so much sheer joy. The moments of refusing to stay with Dan in his office when I left her there and just standing and staring at the door needed to be remembered. When she was little and would lose her mind every time she saw my son Evan at school, convinced that he would rescue her and it was time to party were moments of joy. The time that she escaped from my office only to round a corner and run into Evan, who thwarted her plan and dragged her back to work. I still laugh when I remember the look of betrayal on her face.

Life is hard and messy and sad. We may not be facing the genocide of our people or living enslaved in ancient Persia, but stress lurks around every corner. Let's hold fast to this last lesson from the book of Esther and write these moments of joy on our hearts.

Chapter 24

Whatever Happened to Vashti?

LET'S FINISH OUR STUDY of Queen Esther's life by going back to where her story began, before she ever entered a beauty pageant or caught the eye of a drunken king. Queen Vashti, the original queen, the one who was tossed aside and replaced, is mentioned in the book of Esther less than ten times. Once a mighty queen, she became a footnote easily overlooked until you dig a little deeper into her actual story.

Queen Vashti by all historical accounts was not a rags to riches story like Esther. She was likely from a very powerful family line with an arranged marriage to the king. Vashti would have been raised with the expectation of royalty and the confidence and training to truly be a queen. Jewish transcripts about Vashti vary wildly. The Babylonian Rabbis loathed Vashti, describing her as ugly, immoral, and a hater of Jews. They accuse her of being up to no good, the same as her husband, and imply that she got exactly what she deserved. Songs about Vashti include lyrics accusing her of having a tail or being covered in pimples to explain why she would not appear before the men when summoned. The Erez Israel Rabbis paint her in a more favorable light, as a woman who was married to a dangerous and drunken fool and eventually stood up to him.

Good, bad, or indifferent Vashti plays a larger role in Esther than she receives credit for. Consider this one simple line in Esther 1:9:

"Queen Vashti also gave a banquet for the women in the royal palace of King Xerxes."

Such a small act, hosting a banquet. Why bother even including it?

Because it was a very big deal, indeed. Earlier in the first chapter of Esther we are told that following his 180 day celebration of himself, Xerxes chose to hold a seven day banquet for all of the people in the citadel of Susa. Except that all of the people of Susa didn't really mean all of the people. This extravagant gesture was only for the men. Without verse nine, we would be tempted to believe that all really meant just that: everyone. Were it not for Vashti's hospitality, the women would have been left entirely out of the revelry. We have to assume that the women at this banquet ranged from wives of foreign leaders to commoners whose husbands worked in the citadel. Many of these women had probably never seen the kind of luxury Vashti casually displayed at this banquet. No matter their station in life, these women would have looked to Vashti as a role model. She was the original Instagram influencer and was well aware of her status. Rich or poor, they all must have hung on her every word and absorbed her every gesture.

King Xerxes calling for his wife on the seventh day of the banquet is not as benign as it seems, either. The king had been on what was essentially a 187 day booze bender. I picture him as red faced, slurring his words and appearing to have a bad case of the meat sweats. He has entertained himself and his guests with any number of prostitutes and harem members and his hygiene is probably beyond questionable at this point. Even all of that probably wasn't the tipping point for Vashti. By most accounts, she was very used to having to bite her tongue while her disorderly husband wreaked havoc.

No, the request was not innocuous. On the contrary, it was downright scandalous depending on whose interpretation you'd like to believe. The king was in high spirits and entertaining a rowdy crowd of men when a debate broke out about which region had the most beautiful women, probably bawdy enough to make people blush even by today's standards. Xerxes eventually bangs a fist on the table and summons seven eunuchs to retrieve his Queen so that he may once and for all settle the debate about who has the prettiest wife. Esther 1:11 tells us that he ordered her to wear her royal crown. Some scholars believe that his order was that she appear wearing only her royal crown in order to put herself on full display. Others roll eyes at this suggestion but do agree that she was most likely ordered to appear unveiled.

The annoyance of being dragged away from your girl gang and paraded about like a piece of meat aside, dressed or not, posed a serious issue for Vashti. This is not a case of a vain and spoiled woman refusing to appease her powerful husband. It was against Persian custom for women to appear before a public gathering of men. As a matter of fact, it was wildly against Persian custom and reportedly the only women who did so were prostitutes. The Queen faced degradation and humiliation. Even worse, she knew that she was facing it with a group of women she influenced watching her. If she, the mighty Queen, was willing to accept this, then what kind of greater abuses would the other women later accept believing it was their place?

So, she gambled. She gambled that her drunken husband wouldn't even remember this incident. She gambled that when he sobered up he would be able to listen to reason about why she had no choice but to refuse. She gambled that she could plead to the fact that she was the mother of his oldest son, heir to the throne, and should not be paraded about for his buddies.

That gamble might have paid off if this drunken angry king hadn't decided to immediately consult his fellas to see how this should be handled. These wimps convinced the king that if he let Vashti get away with a slight of this magnitude all of the women everywhere would live in uprising forever. No man would ever know peace again. They recommended she never be allowed in his presence again and that she be replaced with a better (read: more obedient) queen. Probably still drunk, Xerxes dispatched criers to all parts of the land to announce that Vashti had been deposed and that all men were the rulers of their homes.

What a wine and testosterone fueled debacle.

When homeboy sobered up and calmed down, he realized what he had done. The Bible tells us that he remembered Vashti. This probably does not mean that he remembered that he once had a wife, but that he missed her and remembered the things about her that he loved. He remembered with sadness, possibly remorse, probably regret. The law of the land was that once the king made a decree it could not be taken back, no matter how inane or how hammered and mad said king was in the moment. He had completely written off his first wife, possibly his first love, the mother of his child, and the woman that he once found so attractive that he passionately argued she was the most beautiful in the world.

While this seems to have very little to do with the story of Esther, other than paving the way for a new queen, it may just lay the foundation for Esther's interaction down the road. When Esther appeared in his court without invitation the King's heart was soft and he asked what she needed. Is it possible that he was more tolerant of a lapse in royal etiquette and procedure having already rashly lost one woman he loved? A few days later when Esther revealed not only Haman's plot but her own Jewishness and the King saw what he believed was Haman compromising her integrity he reacted quickly on her behalf. Was this because his heart was so softened and protective of the woman he loved that he was willing to risk public embarrassment by admitting the betrayal of his closest advisor to keep her and her people safe? The king who once banished his own wife and firmly stomped the kingdom's women back into what his buddies thought was their place without a second thought was now choosing a woman over male friends and political alliances.

Had the King really learned his lesson? Was Vashti's removal not in vain and deserving of being more than just a brief footnote?

Here is what I love about the parallels of these two women. Now, some of this may be conjecture and I may get schooled by smarter adulty-adults down the road but stay with me for a moment. Let's get warm and fuzzy together. Vashti is often referred to as the forgotten queen. She lived a big life only to be reduced to mentions in a book named for her successor and to have her moral character hotly debated during the Jewish festival of Purim. Yet she could have been completely forgotten, totally wiped from history altogether. It is believed that good old Mordecai wrote what became the book of Esther. I like to believe that there was collaboration with his Queen as he wrote, probably much more productive than the collaboration I've had while writing this with my own Esther.

They could have chosen to leave Vashti out of the story, chosen to not admit that Esther was actually a second wife. Esther could have been threatened that the woman she replaced was so incredibly beautiful that her new husband had once wanted nothing more than to show her off to make other men jealous. Those are big shoes to fill. It would have been so tempting to just quietly allow herself to go down in history as the first queen of Xerxes, the super pretty one who was also very wise and courageous. Who wants to admit that they were chosen in what was basically a royal dating game and they were replacing a well known supermodel?

I think her inclusion was carefully thought out, that the cousins were giving a nod to her courage to stand up to the king and also paying homage to what her sacrifice did to the king's heart down the road. I also believe (Forgive me scholars if I am wrong. And also, don't tell me because I am really excited about this.) that they wanted to carefully record not only Vashti's bravery but to set the precedent of acknowledging those that went before us. Whatever traction we've gained in life, if we are honest, we gained because someone who came before stooped low enough that we might step up onto their shoulders and into the future.

As people, we have a duty to look out for each other, to be grateful to those that stooped so that we could stand on their shoulders, and to stoop so that those behind us may also get ahead. As Esther the Comfort Dog caught on and I was flooded with requests for information, guidance, and advice I made sure to take every call, answer every email, and accommodate every appointment request, often to the fury of my husband who was convinced I was missing a marketing opportunity and a chance to further my career. I felt driven to freely share as much as I could with as many people as possible, not because I am noble but because I am grateful. I am grateful to every mentor along the way who took the time to help me grow. I am grateful to Brad, Jeannette, and Jill for their investment in my wild plans, grateful to a school community who embraced and supported a little dog, grateful for my friends who dragged me through it, grateful to my husband and kids for always being a soft place to land, and grateful to God for the wild and abundant blessings He has given me.

Sharing my blessings with others doesn't mean less blessings for me, it actually works quite the opposite. There is always more room at the table, but there is no place for unhealthy competition. That's how God's abundance works, the love and support that we give others wildly multiplies. So along the way I helped everyone I could and I cheered every time another facility dog popped up in a school. I hope every school in the country has a dog or two before long.

Oh, and one last loose end. If you are worried about Vashti and what became of her then let me leave you with a happy ending. It's traditionally assumed that a queen who was deposed was either killed, shipped back to her people, or just banished somewhere in the royal courts to mill about with the concubines and avoid the king. Now there is no record of Vashti being killed. Honestly, in the King's drive to establish total male dominance in the hours following his decree I have to think that a good old fashioned hanging of the queen would have been recorded in painstaking detail. Vashti is historically believed to have been from a royal family in Babylon. There is no record of her popping back up there or anywhere else in history. There is also no dramatic shipping off of the deposed queen, which seems a little sketchy for a book that obviously relishes hugely dramatic moments and thrives on emotional reveals.

Here is where we do find Vashti in ancient records; her son with Xerxes, Artaxerxes, assumed the throne at his passing and Vashti is recorded as the Queen Mother. It is likely that she spent her time before becoming the Queen Mother in the king's courts, avoiding him and hopefully reaping the admiration of the women around her who would have remembered her brave stand, eventually regaining all of the influence that she had lost. Patience means wait your turn, for in God's time everything does indeed unfold.

CPSIA information can be obtained
at www.ICGtesting.com
Printed in the USA
FSHW021502031120